The Truth Tuning Toolkit

A Series of

Exercises

for the **Mortal**

Mind Mechanism

Steven Joshua

authorHOUSE®

AuthorHouse™
1663 Liberty Drive
Bloomington, IN 47403
www.authorhouse.com
Phone: 1-800-839-8640

First published by AuthorHouse 3/10/2011

ISBN: 978-1-4567-5623-9 (sc)
ISBN: 978-1-4567-5624-6 (hc)

Library of Congress Control Number: 2011908036

Printed in the United States of America

This book is dedicated to you,
the reader, God's Creation -- the Beloved of God.
Steven Joshua

TABLE OF CONTENTS

Application #1 -- Orientation

This is an introduction tool and the first element to a set of exercises. This application defines the work place of this book. There are no exercises in this first element of the series.

Exercise Series Introduction

A definition for truth used in this book is, "laws by which something works." This 'toolkit' gives you numerous applications demonstrating to you how your mind works; and, how it works along a specific set of truths/laws.

You do not have to know what these laws/truths are. Just as, you do not have to know what gravity is to walk. You just have to apply it.

The exercises in this series are abridged exercises or labs extracted from the pages of *I AM A I, Unfolding the Flower*. This exercise set is offered for those who are looking for the practical how-to mystically orientated exercises without having to endure ponderous philosophies.[1]

Be advised though, these exercises do serve as an introduction to some ancient ideas that pervade established 'working' mystical or spiritual schools of thought – ponderous philosophies.

The parent book *I AM A I* presents a comprehensive cohesive thought system using a mathematical and scientific based paradigm. The 'lab' for the mystic science textbook (and these exercises) is you-behind-the-eyes and between-your-ears, your mind. The exercises from the Toolkit have connections within *I AM A I*'s holistic paradigm. Consequently, there are footnotes in this exercise series referring to *I AM A I* text.

For those who are interested in such things as God, internal work, the nature of you and the universe, etc., it is suggested you read *I AM A I* text and read these exercises in their entirety.

And, as stated previously, your knowledge of the thought system/construct of *I AM A I* text is not important to your applications of these exercises. You do not have to know gravitational physics in order to walk. Nor...do you have to be an engineer to drive a car. **Absolute** – Spiritual -- and **Actual** – physical -- reality[2] truth/laws work when applied independent of belief.

---

[1] The majority of the theory that is presented is for an overview into what you are doing. (Such as in the *11th* and *12th* applications in the series, which are all theory.)
[2] *I AM A I*, Chapter 4.2, 'What's Reality Papa?'

In addition, these truths/laws can withstand any amount of questioning; questioning gravity has no affect on gravity.[3]

You do not have to believe in Bernoulli's principle to fly a paper airplane.[4] You just have to apply it. That is what this series of exercises is about; to get you to apply specific concepts so that you can see that your mind is more than a two-dimensional sheet of paper; when it can be a three-dimensional airplane or a stork.

The exercises in this series of applications involve the basic mechanics of your being, how your mind/heart operates. Because of this, the exercises are generic enough to enhance and be adaptable to most 'working' religious and mystical philosophies. Therefore, taking some of the concepts presented in this book, you may develop some useful personal applications of your own from these exercises using your present personal philosophy.

The exercises are only introductions to what you can do; they serve as introductions to some concepts – a springboard. Where the 'lab' applications take you, is up to you. The intention of writing them here is to just pass some concepts on to you, to open up your mind to what you can do.

The 'bottom line' is you are not your mortal mind.[5] Your mortal mind is your vehicle in your body just as your body is your vehicle in the physical world. You are neither.[6] Just as you learned coordination of your body, it makes perfect sense that you learn coordination of the mind as well.

This exercise series gives you numerous tools to help you with this.

Employing the following exercises, there will be an effect on you. What that effect might be is contingent on numerous variables.[7]

Some of these variables are:

o   your intention behind doing the exercise
o   your attachment to what you are doing
o   the amount of one-point focus (remembering your intention and constancy of exercise execution)

---

[3] It is untruth – ~~truth~~, illusion, and delusion that cannot stand honest questioning. They fall apart before it.
[4] You could question Bernoulli's Principle from now to 'doomsday' and it will have no effect on it.
[5] A mind with temporal and spatial limits
[6] One recurring premise is there is only One Mind outside temporal/spatial limits
[7] *I AM A I*, Chapter 5, Formula of Effectiveness

- how much truth and ~~truth~~[8] is programmed in your mind the time of the operation
- repetition

The value of many of these exercises becomes apparent when applied over an extended time window and with some repetition. This is representative of mind programming changes.

For those of you who have previous experience or knowledge of mysticism or spiritual disciplines, you will find that some of the elements present in the Toolkit's applications are found in mystical exercises that have been taught for thousands of years.

The Peace of God is with you; it never left you. You are asleep to it. And…however you use this toolkit, remember:

⇨ There is a God. (And…is just as present with you as you read this as gravity is)

⇨ Whatever you give to Love, it will use.

⇨ Love is not exclusive.

---

[8] In this text and *I AM A I*, the opposite of a word is the word with lines through it. For example; untruth is ~~truth~~; unreal is ~~real~~; or not love is ~~love~~, etc. This detail helps illustrate the point of one term being an opposite.

Application #1A – Truth Recognition

This tool illustrates the effect truth has in your mind. This entry continues from the previous element – the introduction. It elaborates on the definition of the 'laboratory' or the area of application of this series. In addition, this exercise introduces to you how truth affects your mind, when Truth is present in your mind.

Exercise 1A – Truth recognition, ring that bell!

Be advised, this exercise is the beginning of the first chapter and opens up *I AM A I* text; consequently, this exercise is orientated to somebody reading that text.

However, this application is relevant to any spiritual or philosophical treatise/dissertation that you read/hear; and, that treatise/dissertation has truth in it. The effect will be the same; therefore, this exercise would be applicable then.

A mystic works with metaphysical laws just as a technician works with physical laws. The laboratory for the exercises in these applications is you-behind-the-eyes or you-between-the-ears – your mind. Here is an example of how this will work.

To paraphrase a quote from the Buddha, you are not to believe anything you read, hear, or see in writing unless something deep down inside you quietly responds and says; "Yes, that's true." It does not matter if you think it may lead to some kind of divine revelation or come from a Divine source. Do not believe it unless something quietly responds deep inside you – a quiet yes. Quietly means; there is no emotional content. Emotion may occur after the 'event', and the 'event' itself occurs without emotion.

Truth, being the laws of Creation, is at the very core of our being. When we hear a symbolic reference to it, our mind makes the connection to Truth and something deep inside us responds. This can be looked upon as a form of sympathetic resonance.

Now and then, *I AM A I* will refer to this quiet response as 'truth ringing' or 'truth bell' inside you. If any information from this text comes along and that bell does not immediately ring, let it go for now. You may however, want to set the information aside on a shelf within you and wait; do not make any judgments. It could be your perceptions are not open enough for that Truth to enter.

'Higher' Truths will not be perceived unless some 'lower' truths are perceived. For example, it is recommended to teach basic math operations (+, -, ÷, x, etc.), before you teach trigonometry. After an individual learns the requisite math operations, then trigonometry is possible.

If you choose to use this information in its originally intended class format, get a notebook. The inside of the notebook cover should be divided into four parts. Each quarter has a different label. One label would be *In*, one label would be *Out*, one label would be *Mine*, and one label would be *After*.

What do these labels mean? Please refer to Figure 1-1. Whenever that 'truth bell' rings within you from something inside a book, you would make a slash mark under *In*. If you heard something outside the

Figure 1-1 Keeping Record

book that rang that bell, you would make a mark in the *Out* box. When you realize something inside yourself, by yourself, and the bell rings; then you would make a mark under *Mine*. *After* was for when you were done with the book and the notebook may become a journal.

It is understood that what you are being asked to recognize is ever so subtle. And…there are some indications that this event has been occurring consistently:

❑ When continually hearing truth, the consciousness change in the hearer can be interesting. This consciousness change expresses itself in different ways. One way can be the listener agrees with every word spoken, perhaps accompanied with a sense of peace and wholeness; and, is unable to remember what was said.

This consciousness change can occur to such a degree; that even though the listener agrees with everything being said, they will not be able to remember what was said. They may just have an idea of the general context. They only know; they agreed with what was said.

❏ A reading symptom of truth presence in the mind that appears is similar to hearing the truth. You are absorbed, agree with everything read, and cannot remember what is being read.

In both cases, higher priority mental operations (cognition and knowledge) are taking precedence over lower priority mental operations (memory).[9] The truth ringing mechanism can interfere with the reading mechanism.

❏ Another reading symptom is when reading truth, the consciousness change can become like a rain on the face analogy. A light rain on the face may feel refreshing, and yet, most people can only take so much of it. Too much rain can feel overwhelming.

One problem with this last example of reading truth is a tendency to put the book down. Usually, this is done to absorb what has been read. If _I AM A I_ is doing its job right, you may be setting the book down on a regular basis. This, in turn, can make that book slow reading.

The main idea of this exercise application is to get you to be familiar with the truth-ringing concept; that an event occurred within you, to feel it, and to learn to recognize it.

For you, the reader, a goal of the exercise may be achieved if you had a pad of paper and a pencil next to you as you are reading a spiritual or philosophical text. Every time you read anything in the text and there is a resonance or _response_ within you, make a hash mark on the pad. By the time you reach 10 to 15 marks, you may have an idea or a feel of this _response_ mechanism to truth. This exercise's purpose will be achieved as long as you recognize 'something' occurred.

It may not be important to know or to indicate what the concept or the thought was. Just that you recognized it happened. You can write it down if you want. However, within an oral class format it could become counter-productive to learning; it splits the focus.

The main intention of this application is to get you to recognize your own mechanism, how you _respond_ to truth, or how truth affects you...deep inside. The _response_ is the important concept; that which keyed the _response_ is of lesser importance for this application.

---

[9] _I AM A I_, Chapter 4

When this exercise series is used as a personal self-help, the _Out_ and _Mine_ boxes are equivalent to keeping a journal for anything. (In addition, it is recommended that you keep a journal or notebook for this set of exercises; however, it is not absolutely necessary.)

Because you probably will not be walking around with a notebook, the _Out_ box may not be marked until you come back to the notebook. ("I heard something 'heavy' today.") For this exercise, only 5-10 hash marks are required in the _Out_ box.

Again, the idea here is to recognize an event occurred inside you. A later exercise will cover _Mine_. *Application 4* will introduce to you how you can perceive your own truths and possibly 'ring your own bell'.

Again, this exercise is applicable to any writings and/or dialogue or monologue that has truth within it.

This application is to:
➢ **Accumulate 10 - 15 hash marks in the In box.**
➢ **5-10 each in the Out box and the Mine box.**
➢ **After 20 hash marks, you could stop because you may be somewhat familiar with this quiet sense.**

To summarize this exercise, your mind is the 'lab' and you are asked to recognize an event occurred in the 'lab'. Do not accept any theory from this text (or any other source) unless there is a quiet response inside you. This also means do not summarily reject the idea either. The idea is to cultivate a 'watching and waiting' attitude to the text and your response to that text.

17

Application #2 – Not Doing

This is a tool that helps maintain an effective working environment. The first two application entries defined the workplace for this series. This tool helps reduce ~~truth~~ extension/creation within your mind.

Exercise 2 – No talking, the sound of silence

When teaching in a class format, this exercise is easy to state. There is to be no talking about your <u>personal experiences</u> (from doing the exercises, reading the textbook, or while participating in the class) with anyone. The only exceptions are if talking fits within the class format (exercise feedback, meditation effects, questions, etc.)

You can talk about content and ideas presented. <u>You are not to talk about your personal experiences from exercise applications</u>.

From 'you the reader' standpoint, this application is a little harder to state. This exercise can be stated as; do not share any personal experiences you have from doing the exercises.[10] You can describe to people the exercises or concepts in the text. However, keep your personal experiences and perceptions to yourself. Do not talk about that which happens when you do these applications. You can write about your experiences in a notebook or journal. However, do not show your notebook or journal or any entries in your journal to anyone (for as long as you are doing the exercises).

There are a multitude of reasons why the silence. Some of these reasons are:

- It keeps you from making some programming choices
- It helps maintain the disinterested interest (non-attachment) necessary for the success of the *ESP* exercises (*Applications 11 and 12*).
- It relates to a Formula of Effectiveness in Chapter 5, *I AM A I*.
- It hinders you from making premature judgments around a subject matter that you are still learning and have not yet finished learning
- It also relates to the To Keep Silent rule of magic in Chapter 9, *I AM A I*.

To keep things simple, look at it this way. These exercises are for a science course and the 'lab' for this course is your mind – you behind-the-eyes and between-the-ears.

Look at your mind as being a laboratory environment. Physically, for a set of experiments within a laboratory environment to work, specific

---

[10] or reading *I AM A I* text

conditions must be maintained within that laboratory environment. This also applies metaphysically. Talking about personal experience affects the laboratory environment within you – your mind's programming -- and therefore can affect the outcome of some of these applications.

Talking is an act of creation – extending an idea -- and it is a choice (both of these are covered in detail in _I AM A I_ text[11]). Every choice you make will have an affect on your mind's programming.

Look at this application as a shotgun approach to maintaining pristine 'lab conditions'. It is a crude way of keeping you from making some specific choices.

This exercise is also an introduction to the concept of 'not doing' something can be as important as 'doing' something. What would be your intention for speaking? Could it be your saying, "Look what I did! Look what I did!" This is listening to your pride or ego. These qualities can hinder the success of future exercises, _Especially ESP_. It can also foster attachments.

The bottom line is; any experiences you have are between you and your Creator/ix -- Love. It really is not anybody's business except yours. An Infinite/Eternal Loving God can customize everybody's spiritual curriculum to each mortal – finite/temporal -- mind's needs. What you may have to learn at this moment, may not be what the person next you has to learn at this moment.

This assignment can be translated as:
➤ **_"Keep silent" about what experiences you have; what you feel; or, your perceptions involving the results of these applications in this exercise series. This is done until you are finished with this set of exercises – the book._**

> *"Those who know, do not talk*
> *Those who talk, do not know."*
> _Tao te Ching_

---
[11] Chapter 4

19

Application #3 – Being Creative

This is an artwork tool that illustrates meditation concepts. This exercise is an introduction to the concept of one-point focus on an event – meditation -- by doing artwork; and, it has you make a meditation aid. In addition, in this application you are making another tool for *Application 9B -- Affirmation Chanting.*

Exercise 3 – Artwork, getting artsy-fartsy

In this application, you are to do some artwork; you are to make your own mandala or yantra. In the back of this book, you will find a set of drawings that can help you.[12]

⇒ One part of that set contains templates for making your own mandala with tracing paper – **Concerning the Templates**.
⇒ The other part of the set of drawings contains mandalas that were made from the mandala template designated *5 (easy)* -- **Concerning the Pre-drawn Figures**. These figures are arrayed throughout the book as examples, with various shadings to show different effects. These pre-drawn figures are also in the back of the book.

A mandala is a geometric piece of art that symbolizes the universe. Therefore, technically, a more accurate term for these figures would be a yantra.[13]

---

[12] The drawings are in the larger format *I AM A I* index as well.
[13] Yantra: A geometric meditation aid

Doing this artwork serves as an introduction to a one-point focus – meditation -- and the artwork itself will be used later with an affirmation chant.

Since you are asked to make your own custom mandala, symbols (relevant to your intention and philosophy) may be inserted into <u>some</u> of the pictures.

A note about sketching and shading

Sketching is for people who cannot draw. You need a line, know you cannot draw it exactly, so you draw a bunch of little lines, and their accumulation presents the line you want (hopefully).

The same can be said with shading a drawing. Start lightly; and that which looks to you could be darker, lightly go over it again and again and...until you are satisfied.

Concerning the Templates

The templates provided are computer drawings of a mathematical construction using the proportions of π and ϕ -- pi and the Golden Section[14] (or Golden Mean). Because these are naturally occurring proportions; if you are going to create something, you may as well use these proportions as a structure or as something to build on.

If not for aesthetic reasons, do it because of the resonant capabilities of like mathematics.[15] Because the templates and mandalas created are based on the Golden Section, they can make some very esthetic hypnotic figures -- something that can suck your vision in and keep it there.

Templates *5 (easy)* and *5 (hard)* are based on the pentagram geometric construction that is in a Euclidian geometry book.[16] The templates *5 (easy)* and *5 (hard)* are the circles that are a result of using the golden section with π, with a few extra circles and lines added.

Templates *4* and *8* are arranged to separate a circle into 4 or 8 sections respectively. Templates *6* and *12* divide a circle into 6 and 12 equal parts respectively. The pattern is the same with templates *7* and *14*. All these figures still use ϕ and π.

You can use one of the provided computer templates to create a customized structure of your own. To do so, take a piece of tracing paper and put it over a template. Then start, for example, with whatever line catches your eye and darken it with a pencil on the tracing paper. Pick out shapes that you see to trace and draw those out on the tracing paper.

---

[14] $(1+\sqrt5)/2$, Chapter 1 of *I AM A I*

[15] Chapter 1 of *I AM A I*

[16] The Golden Section can be used to divide a circle into 10 equal parts.

You know you are going to make a figure, so start picking out patterns, and just follow lines. You can make a mandala squarish, anything you want. For example, Templates *4* and *8* can generate a square-like mandala/yantra.

This particular version of the assignment consists of tracing out four different mandalas with pencil using whatever templates you want. Whatever lines your eye picks out under the tracing paper; you follow with the pencil. You do not have to do it 'this way', or 'that way' or any particular way.

You can 'putz' around and do this in front of the TV, listening to music, commuting on a train, or something. Go over with ink the ones that you like the best.

Please note: not drawing a line is as, or more, important than drawing a line. An example is in some of the demonstrated figures -- **Concerning the Pre-drawn Figures**. Where there are several lines meeting, it was left open to avoid a busy-ness at that point.

The rose pattern (mandala 9)[17] came out of *5 (easy)*. That was to be the logo for a Mystic Arts class. Numerous mandalas where done, before the author finally started to see and create patterns that the author really liked.

After you trace some lines, and have some outlines of several basic mandalas, make copies of each mandala. Then go back with pencil and start shading the copies to your preference. The author found, when using these figures for the later chanting exercise -- *Exercise 9B, Affirmation Chanting*, that black and white figures work better than color figures. The black and white simplifies the amount of data coming in to the mind. The color ones can be distracting.

Examples of shaded mandalas are laced throughout this book. This artwork exercise can be just the beginning point for more mystical artwork if you wish to take this further.

Concerning the Pre-drawn Figures
If all this seems like too much work (which it is a lot), the pre-drawn mandalas in the back of this book are available to be copied, shaded, or altered by you. It is for that purpose they are there. They can save you some work and still help illustrate the one-point focus concept used later.

Alternatively, for the later chanting exercise, you can also research mandalas and find four different other figures you would like to work with;

---

[17] back of book

mandalas that are in keeping with your personal philosophy. Remember though, the figure you choose must not be so 'busy' that it distracts. This may counteract the effect of the later affirmation exercise.

And…if you pick a picture or symbol (as opposed to making one), you may miss the one-point focus reference used later.

This application consists of:
- ➤ **To make four different mandalas, one to be used later; or, find four mandalas that you can use.**
- ➤ **Construct at least one geometric mandala or yantra <u>without</u> symbols, words, figures, animals, etc. and keep it purely black and white.**

Application #4 – That Which Is Around You

This tool helps you access the truth around you by using mundane objects. With this application, you are introduced to the idea of perceiving comprehensive truths using mundane objects that are around you. You do this by thinking in parallels.

Exercise 4 – Truth perception (or parallel parking)

This is a long-term exercise and involves one truth a day for an extended period – 10 weeks to a year. This 'truth' is to be entered into a notebook or journal. This 'truth' is not to be something you read or you are told. It is to be picked up from an everyday object around you.

This application can help give your limited mortal mind another dimension. Working with parallel concepts allows for a broader scope of perception. (Our mind tends to do patterns and parallels cross referencing in the 'background' as a data referencing device.)

In this exercise, you will be involved with mentally jumping parallels through truth perception and cognition using something around you. You will use mundane objects to see universal concepts.

This is how do you do this exercise. Pick an object, any object around you. Examine it and ask questions.

Ask: Who?, What?, Where?, When?, etc.[18] Then ask, "What is this like?"

Pick an object that is around you! Break it down in to function and ask questions like who, what, where when, how, etc. After answering some of these questions, make a parallel to something that is much grander or bigger than the original object. You are to take an everyday object and parallel it in to Life, People, the World...

The end product – what goes in the journal -- should appear something like; "A _____ is like a _____. Because of _____."
Your explanation should be only about two sentences.

Some common parallels that may prove useful may be:

- Light: almost any thing dealing with light parallels to truth, knowledge, or education.
- Air: parallels into change, life, or people.
- Water: can parallel into life, softness, people, or flexibility.
- Food: can make parallels into learning, growth, people, and survival.
- Fire or chemical reactions: make great metaphysical parallels into change, both passive and active, or people's passion.
- Tools and utensils: can parallel the human condition.
- Anything that deals with the earth or soil: can parallel into that which is solid, basic, or unmovable.

The author learned this exercise as a high school sophomore in Mr. Zehren's English class. In the class, the author had to do one truth a day and put it down in a notebook. The author had Mr. Zehren everyday (5 days a week) for two semesters; so, the author at fifteen years old had to do this exercise for nine months.

Being lazy, the author seldom did his until he got to class. He must have gotten over thirty truths looking at or through the classroom windows. Some examples of this are:

❑ Some people are like windows and let knowledge or truth into our lives.

---

[18] Be careful of 'Why?', because you can always ask 'Why not?'.

- The glass and the teachers teaching in the classroom.
- Some people are like windows and let fresh air in our lives.
    - Opening the window and the 'changes' we like. (laughter, joy, 'warm fuzzy', etc.)
- Some people are like shades and block the light/knowledge coming to us.
    - Pulling down the shades for *AV* purposes and some unpleasant inter-personal interactions.
    - When the light is blocked from without us, perhaps it is to have us watch the movie within us.
    - If this is a cosmic lesson plan, whose hand really controls the shade?
        - ❖ The teacher directing a student to close the shade.
        - ❖ Watching the internal movie.

Be advised that adding modifiers like *some* or *sometimes* can make your truths more accurate or comprehensive. For example, saying, "Some people are like windows..." is more accurate than, "People are like windows..." Not everybody is like this. In saying *some*, there will always be someone somewhere acting like this (if not just a parent to a child). These modifiers can help make your 'truth' more accurate and comprehensive.

The author did this exercise with another person and this is how it turned out.

Pick an object! The person the author demonstrated this to picked an on-off switch on an in-line power supply and amplifier mounted on the cord of a microphone.[19] The power supply uses a battery. It has a little clip on it so it can mount on the belt or shirt.

(*Anything around you can be used for this exercise*! Whatever you do use, give it the **K.I.S.S.** [**K**eep **I**t **S**imple **S**tupid]. Do not try to have an explanation for everything at once.)

Once you pick an object and mentally examine it, start looking for parallels.

To begin, start asking questions about the object. Who, what, when, where, why, how, sequencing of relationships, etc., and make a list.

---

[19] We were recording this at the time.

For example:

- ❏ Who would use this?
  - Somebody who wishes to record.
- ❏ Who would make that switch?
  - Somebody who wishes to eat.
- ❏ How does it work or what is it?
  - It is something that aids the microphone in the transmission of sound to a tape recorder.
  - It is a go/no-go device
- ❏ When is it used/not used?
  - When you wish to record on a tape recorder.
  - You do not use it when you want to play the tape recorder; it might give feedback.
- ❏ Without that on-off switch, amplifier, or battery, the mike system will not work.

The next thing to do is examine some relationships. The microphone is recording, but what is it recording?

The mike can record a myriad of things: music, words and discussions, or nonsense and noise. At the time, the microphone was being used to record the author's words. The mike, switch, and amplifier are totally neutral in terms of what they let through to the tape recorder or not.

The sound is coming from the source, through the medium of the air. The mike takes the sound, changes it to electrical energy, which travels down the wire into this battery back and amplifier. It is amplified by the battery (which is engaged by the switch) and then is picked up by the tape recorder. The mike, amplifier, on-off switch, and cord are a whole transducer assembly. It transduces sound to electricity. What the on-off switch and amplifier are doing is allowing the change of electrical signals (created by sound), to go from the mike to the tape recorder; again, it is a go/no-go device.

The object was mentally dissected. What does it do, how is it used, and what is it for? Next, is to jump into parallels. Ask what else does this, or what is this like? For example, what else acts a go/no-go device between an amplifier between what is done on one end, as the mike (a transducer), and how it is received on the other, as the tape deck?

The mike and the tape deck have a specific relationship, one is sending and one is receiving. The mike's inline amplifier switch is there to facilitate that. If we look at the mike, amplifier, and tape deck as being all in one person, then we can say our grasp of language acts as an amplifier switch or transducer of what we hear to ideas we recognize. This go/no-go device is like your grasp of language.

When it was said in Chapter 1, "Some of the squared legs equals the square of the hippopotamus."[20] That may have been nonsense to you until it was explained. Your grasp of language translates what comes in and determines what is recognized. There is a flow from the mike (author's words), through an amplifier (language/perception), to the tape deck (cognition).[21] "Oh, I got it." Click! One go/no-go device facilitates a flow of electrons; the other facilitates a flow of ideas.

Who or what can also act like an on/off switch to the flow of ideas? How about a language translator; someone who allows the flow of ideas between two languages?

So it can be said, *"A language translator is like a switch – a go/no-go device -- to the flow of complex ideas between peoples with different languages."*

Because, without a language translator, complex ideas do not flow. Ideas flow with a language translator.

That is only one parallel to this mike/amplifier/recorder go/no-go array. It is possible to have other parallels.

As was just done; extend the everyday object into comprehensive generalities, things that tend to be all encompassing: Life, God, humanity, growth, people, etc. The more inclusive or comprehensive the result, the better.

This exercise will help facilitate the 'ring' necessary for part of the first exercise -- the *Mine* box.[22] Through this exercise, you can generate that 'ring' inside you.

That previous mentioned truth 'ringing' is also facilitated as you, the individual, begin to assemble the truths perceived, and applying them.[23] A mystical operator or metaphysical student's goal should be making their truth matrix similar to the Absolute Truth Matrix, rebuilding their human matrix – mortal mind. Or, more accurately, reprogramming their existing human mind/matrix so it is similar to the Absolute Truth Mind/Matrix – create common tangent points. Having their matrix store 'absolutes' they perceive, helps facilitate this.[24]

---

[20] Pythagorean Theorem

[21] *I AM A I*, Chapter 4.4 and 4.5, The Human Matrix - *Storages* and The *Perceptual Lens Array*

[22] *Application 1A*

[23] *I AM A I*, Chapter 4.8, Ring My Bell

[24] *I AM A I*, Chapter 9 and 10

A review of this exercise: you select an object and you examine it for what, where, when, how, and the sequencing of events that determine its use. Just examine for the facts that you see in it.

Okay. Suppose we have a container with us (a plastic one-liter container with a snap top) and it holds water at that moment, but it can hold other things. It's made of plastic; has a removable top,

Assuming the liquid is for human consumption (which is what it was used for at that moment in time), the liquid -- no matter what it is -- has water in it. The liquid in the container could be plain water as the one the author had in his hand, juice with water and other nutrients in it, or wine. One way or another, whether it is water or juice or whatever, the container is holding a liquid with a life-giving element (water).

The exercise is for you to look at it, determine whatever it is for, and in the end, jump parallels into your perception of life. So…what, in the human system, is life giving or is a vessel for life giving? (The parallels can go in multiple directions. For this example, it will be narrowed down and given a direction.)

What is it or what something is necessary for peoples -- as a whole, something we need within us, outside us, for our learning or growth? What else is like this vessel that holds water? This -- the water -- is something that is absolutely necessary whereas the vessel can hold a liquid that is not absolutely necessary, like wine. So, what in our lives is as a vessel that can be used for something we absolutely need, or just to hold something that we use and do not absolutely need?

How about knowledge? It holds truth (or truth applications[25]).

In one way, knowledge (truth applications) based on **Absolute** and **Actual** reality[26] are truths essential for survival, and we cannot do without them. Otherwise, we would not be able to walk, talk, eat, and survive.

Yet, though there is knowledge that is based on Absolute and Actual Truths – essential, there are truths that make up some of the **Individual**, **Consensual**, and **Imaginary** realities and are not essential to physical existence. This is knowledge that is based on relative truth applications (language, society, politics, etc.). We can take both in; the fantasy book sitting over there or playing with the computer on the Internet. These are not essential for physical survival within the natural system; and, it is knowledge that we take in.

So we can say, "_Knowledge_ is like a _container_. Some things in our knowledge are necessary to survive while other things held by our knowledge are not essential to survival."

---

[25] _I AM A I_, Chapter 4
[26] _I AM A I_, Chapter 4.2, 'What's Reality Papa?'

With this exercise, hopefully you can see how you can take anything, jump into parallels, and you see something way beyond a mere jug of water.

Now, as to your categorizing of the truths that you pick up from these parallels; after a while, you will notice some parallels apply to all or everybody. In addition, you will see other parallels will apply to some cases and not to others.

Some of the determining factors will be:

- your wording,
- individual perceptions, where you are 'standing' when you 'look' at something
- what truth is stored in your knowledge already.

Next to each truth formulated in this exercise, mark a category you perceive the truth to be. The categories are *absolute* (*A*), *unknown* (*?*), or *relative* (*R*).

A $\Rightarrow$ The *absolute* category is when the truth appears to apply to everything applicable in a situation or scenario.

R $\Rightarrow$ The *relative* category is when you see it applying to some things, while not to others.

? $\Rightarrow$ The *unknown* category is when you are not sure.

If you find one exception to a truth in the *absolute* category, it becomes a *relative* truth or possibly a (*?*). Use the geometric postulate analogy: if one exception is found to a postulate, it ceases to be a postulate.

However, exceptions must be examined just as carefully as the original truth. What may be an exception in one way may not be an exception when perceived in another way. What you 'see' will be dependent on where you are 'standing' when you look at it.

For example: what you may <u>see</u> as an exception may be due to how you are perceiving -- looking at it. The changing of your perception can cause the exception to disappear. The exception becomes a special case.

Be like the 'fair witness' concept, presented in the book *Stranger in a Strange Land*.[27] When a woman Ann, who was a fair witness, was asked the color of the house on the hill, she turned to Jubal and said, "It's white

---

[27] A science fiction book by Robert Heinlein, Copyright 1961... A fair witness was trained in observation to such an extent that whatever a fair witness said happened, was accepted in a court of law as fact.

29

on this side, Jubal." Be objective. Recognize what you see is on 'this side'. Just because one side of a house is white does not mean the whole house is white. Then look around to the other side, it might be black.

24 ounces, 700 milligrams (markings on the plastic container).

Like the plastic container, changing where you stand changes what you see. On one side is metric measure and it says 700 milliliters, which is speaking one language. Looking on the other side, the markings say 24 ounces -- which is speaking another measure language, and both languages have to do with the same thing, volume. Two symbol systems, one is from Napoleon and the other from English; and yet, the two symbol systems are talking about the same thing -- quantity.

So...it can be said:

The same knowledge can be expressed through multiple symbol systems – languages.

Be like the 'fair witness'. By being open and not shut anything out, you are observing like the 'fair witness'. Being honest with yourself more than anything else; get rid of your preconceived notions, be open. Or..."In the eyes of a child..."

There may be some truths you may not want to believe, or not even want to recognize. We can recognize and not want to believe it. But, we must re-cognize it at least. (Recognized -- re-cognized -- or not, Absolute and Actual Truth still exists.)

That is what is meant by an honest frame of mind, dispassionately. If we refuse to re-know the Truth, it will not do us any good. We must re-know it, re-cognize its existence, if not believe it. Through this the Cognitive Input of our mind programs our *Knowledge*.[28]

Here is the application:
- ➤ *A truth/day taken from an everyday object and to enter it in a notebook or journal for an extended period of time -- ten weeks to a year.*
- ➤ *State what was the original object, and then, state the 'truth' perceived. The format: A/Some _____ is like a _____. Because they both: 2 sentences .*
- ➤ *In the margin before your truth enter the category you perceive it to be in: Absolute, Relative, or ? (you do not know).*
- ➤ *In addition, five slashes are required in the cover of the notebook for the Mine category of Application 1A.*

---

[28] *I AM A I*, Chapter 4, Realities and the Human Matrix

Advantages of this application

There are a multitude of advantages to learning this exercise. Some of the advantages produced by doing this exercise everyday over an extended window of time -- months -- are:

1. Learning to think in parallels adds another dimension to your mind.

This exercise can expand your mortal perceptual window on things. You can see beyond the object at hand, as you begin thinking in parallels.

2. Things become simpler as you start thinking in parallels.

Looking at things, what one sees becomes increasingly complicated: *BTRs*[29] within *BTRs* within *BTRs*..., matrices within matrices within matrices..., mirrors within mirrors within mirrors..., etc.

With so many variables, the diversity can give the mortal brain a cramp. However, once you begin thinking in parallels, things can get simpler instead of more complicated. The similarities and connections can be seen. You can begin to generate a more non-exclusive mind or a mind with Love in it. You can start seeing connections between things.

As stated previously, you are starting to put your human mind/matrix to work and reprogramming it according to the lines of the Absolute Truth Matrix. As the mind becomes increasingly non-exclusive, an individual begins to see more. This effect makes it possible to relate all the information in *I AM A I* (or in spiritual philosophies) into reoccurring themes.

3. Since absolute truth is invulnerable and unchangeable, this exercise can give you a place to 'stand'.

This can be important in a sea of changes. Keeping to absolute truths can be like standing on a rock in troubled seas. This application can be useful when doing *ESP* experiments along with the truthful questioning of an *ESP* event.

In addition, this exercise can be quite helpful for you to understand mundane events (as well as mystical events).

4. This exercise facilitates comprehensive truth storage within the mind.

This is why you categorize. When the fictional character Sherlock Holmes first meets Watson in the story *A Study in Scarlet*,[30] Watson and Holmes are students together at a University. Watson sees that Sherlock Holmes is equivalent to a genius, and is very much learned in a number of different subjects: chemistry, forensics, ballistics, etc. He also learns Holmes is totally ignorant on other subjects like astronomy. This is in an

---

[29] Bubbles of Temporal/spatial Reference, *I AM A I*, Chapter 3
[30] Sir Author Conan Doyle

antithesis of the popular concept of the times (the *enlightened man*).

The *enlightened man* had to know a little bit of everything. Watson asked Holmes, how it is that he could be so learned in one field and completely ignorant of another.

To paraphrase Holmes' response: I look at my mind like an attic. Most people store anything they come across, throw it in their attic, and their attic becomes one big clutter. I choose to store only specific things in my attic. I do not want my attic cluttered.

If a person uses this concept with the Absolute Truth and starts storing in their 'attic' only Absolute Truth – that which they can find no exception to, this lesson will produce results over time.

This exercise can expand your understanding and knowledge base, while simplifying it, as in *Advantage 2* above. Storage of 'absolutes' automatically starts to regulate incoming unknowns to being 'special case' applications of the 'absolutes'.

We can input Absolute Truth into our human matrix. When we use these parallels between metaphysical and physical, we begin to generate an inclusive mind through Truth; Love's Truth is all encompassing – non-exclusive. The more absolutes we input and connect together, the more our human matrix becomes similar to the Truth Matrix.[31] The Truth in our minds – temporal -- will have an affect by aligning itself with the Truth Matrix – eternal -- naturally.

It is the truth in the matrix that defines the matrix. Yet it is the matrix that defines the exhibited properties. Take the molecule H_2O for example. The H_2O molecule has intrinsic qualities. The matrix formed by H_2O may be ice or a snowflake. The water molecule defines two states, both ice and a snowflake.

Another example is carbon. It is the matrix that the carbon molecules are in that defines its exhibited properties. The exhibited properties could be soot, activated charcoal, anthracite coal, or a diamond. Carbon has not changed; only the matrix the carbon is in has changed.

Personal beliefs and philosophies are defined by the truth in the philosophy. Truth defines its own matrix. The philosophies are important in that they help you array the truth within your mind. As new absolute truths are learned, the philosophy must change (to accommodate it). Either that, or be in some form of denial of that truth.

This exercise facilitates truth storage in your mind and has a comprehensive truth matrix assemble within you as you do so.

---

[31] *I AM A I*, Chapter 2.5 - *Postulate 4*, God's Logical Mind is a matrix of Absolute, Eternal Truth.

5.   The "Know the truth and the truth will set you free" mechanism

How does this work? A review of some of *I AM A I* material may be helpful here. In Chapter 2 and Chapter 3, two concepts were introduced:

- ❖ The concepts of infinite and finite or eternal and temporal as being mutually exclusive.
  - ⇒ If something is not infinite, it is finite. If something is not finite, it is infinite.
  - ⇒ If something is not eternal, it is temporal. If something is not temporal, it is eternal.
- ❖ The concept that a logic system can create something alien to that logic system.
  - ⇒ In mathematics, the concepts of division by zero ($^x/_0$) and taking the square root (or even root) of a negative number ($\sqrt{-1}$).
  - ⇒ These two examples are how a complete and comprehensive logic system, which deals with infinities within infinities within infinities...infinitely, can create something that is outside of that logic system.

The postulates and theorems of Chapter 2 focus on an infinite/eternal Mind manifesting a finite/temporal condition; and, it can go the other direction as well. This means, if a finite/temporal mind – mortal mind -- creates something alien to it, that creation will automatically be infinite/eternal – Divine Love -- related in some way.

When a finite/temporal mind – mortal mind -- programs itself with eternals and absolutes, it becomes easier to for that mind to create something that is alien to it or initiates something that 'exits' the mortal mind.

In the bible, it is written that Jesus said, "Know the truth and the truth will set you free." Because Truth is constant, this is just as true now as it was in Jesus' time. Once truths are accumulated, they start appearing in/assembling themselves into matrices they are normally in. Again, as the water molecule defines the nature of a snowflake; so does the nature of the truth define the nature of the thought construct -- philosophy.

When absolute truth starts assembling with other absolute truth (this absolute truth together with this absolute truth together with this absolute truth) within a mortal mind, a 'whirrr click' can occur inside a person; a cognitive jump occurs. This 'whirrr click' (a specific 'ringing' of the individual matrix/mind[32]) is an instant change of a mental/emotional state --

---

[32] 'Ring' as in *Application 1A*.

consciousness. This change tends to be comprehensive in scope when you are dealing with absolutes.

You perceive the truth matrix involved. Any truth you learn regarding that particular subject matter afterward, you can 'see' where or how it 'fits' in the matrix.

This change of state can give a quiet peace and an understanding based on whole concepts of comprehensive truth - a comprehensive *'quiet understanding'*. Alternatively, it can also be an epiphany.

In both cases, the matrix the truth is in becomes part of your individual mind matrix; an alignment occurs.

After this has happened a number of times, and a number of *'quiet understandings'* – comprehensive cognitive jumps -- have been stored in your mental matrix. One *'quiet understanding'* (based on absolute truth) assembles with another *'quiet understanding'*, with another *'quiet understanding'*, and with another *'quiet understanding'*... the 'whirrr click' (the cognitive jump) is going to be a religious experience, independent of whether you believe in God or not.

Because...God is the source of all Absolute Truth. In the end, you are just following the Truth to its Source. So, if you keep on working with comprehensive or Absolute Truth within an honest framework of mind, you are going to end up with a religious experience of some sort, because God is the Source of the Absolute Truth.

Or, in other words, when you start assembling Absolute Truths together, you get these peaceful points of knowledge, which -- when assembled -- bring you to God independent of whether you even believe in God.

Belief in a system is not that important to the process. It is the truths in the thought system that facilitates the process.

<u>What is being described here is a mechanism</u>. This is how the mechanism "Know the truth and the truth will set you free" works.

And be advised, if this type of cognitive jump occurs without a supporting absolute truth matrix in the mortal mind, this cognitive jump can fracture some **Individual** realities.

The ~~truths~~ can dissolve in that mortal mind matrix to such an extent that the mortal mind has a problem functioning for a while.

6. **An old spiritual axiom is. "There is nowhere you need to go to learn the Truth. Everything you need to know is right there in front of you."**
    If you really learn this lesson -- how to think in parallels from a simple common object to something all encompassing, everything you need to know, spiritually and metaphysically, becomes accessible. You only have to be aware and have your eyes open.

Spiritual knowledge becomes assessable to you and it always has been right in front of you in common everyday objects. You just have to look at the object, learn to jump in parallels, and everything really you need to know is there.

God is not hiding anything; everything you need to know is right in front of you.

This application works best when you make no judgments as the objective observer (mentioned previously). Be aware of your ignorance because your ignorance is going to be part of this application.

Application #5 – Resetting the Mind

This is a tool that helps you reset your mind. Here you use a temporal limit of your finite mortal mind to prevent mentation -- thought.

Exercise 5 – Temporal mind limits, surfing the mechanism

Our mind has many mental paths and feedback loops. Because we are dealing with a temporal mind, each path or loop takes 'x' amount of time to occur. Some happen quicker while others take longer to occur. For example, the loop from an Event, to our re-cognition of the Event's existence, to our focusing, and re-cognizing the Event itself (Chart 4-4, N5),[33] takes a specific amount of time. This time lapse can be used.

The Cognitive path is a high priority path. It is a survival path. All mortal minds, including animal minds, have a Cognitive input. It involves the sensory input going into the mind. When it is in constant use, <u>lesser priority mental paths must give way</u>.

---

[33] *I AM A I*, Chapter 4 and Figure 4-4 in the back of this book

This is an eye exercise where you focus on one physical thing and move the eyes quickly from one item to another item. The eyes are on the item long enough that you recognize a perceptual change has occurred, but not long enough for complete recognition of the item to occur. Your eyes do not rest long enough finish the process or to allow any other mind/matrix operation.

Moving the eyes to 'something', the mind/matrix is refocusing until there is re-cognition. After the cognition, a number of mental loops can occur. Moving and refocusing the eyes before the re-cognition loop is complete; calls for a mind refocus. Constantly focusing the eyes on separate things for a period of time means your mind/matrix is constantly refocusing and little ~~truth~~ is chosen during that moment; nor, is a 'subjective event' (thought) allowed to occur. Done quickly enough, no mentation occurs. If you find yourself thinking, you are not moving the eyes fast enough or you're not bringing your focus to bear on the objects.

Because little ~~truth~~ is chosen for a period of time and consequently not dampening the mind/matrix, a slight 'ringing' or a consciousness change occurs.[34]

There is a direct relationship between time length of an empty mind and consciousness change; the longer the time the great the change.[35] (By empty mind, there is choice but very-little-to-zero perceptual input into *Programming*.)

In this application, you are to change your perception input faster than the perception/cognition/knowledge/you loop can operate. You are to change your physical focus faster than your mind/matrix operates. In doing this, 'surfing' the changes in your mind, you are preoccupying the mechanism and very-little-to-zero Choice input enters *Programming*.

You are using the temporal operating limits of your mortal mind/matrix to step out of your usual mental operation.

A result of this operation is; because the Cognitive path is a high priority path, an extended cognitive preoccupation resets the mind. After doing this exercise, your mind starts over. This application automatically disrupts previous mentation.

To do this exercise:
➢ **First, take a moment and notice how you are feeling and the nature of your most recent thought processes.**
➢ **Do this exercise for <u>one minute</u>. Move the eyes to one thing, then to another, then to another...**
➢ **Afterward, take another moment and notice where your 'head is at' – how you feel.**

---

[34] 'Ringing' as in *Application 1A*
[35] *Applications 8-10*

> ➤ **Assignment: Do this exercise for one minute on 10 separate occasions.**
> ➤ **Notice and/or record your change of perceptions/feelings in your journal or notebook.**

This eye exercise can be a tool to manually reset your mind. It causes a reset in your *Programming* storage.

Deep meditation can also cause your mind to reset just like this exercise can manually reset your mind.

The mind resets naturally as well. Naturally, there are numerous ways the mind resets itself:

- One is laughter. A laughter reset involves *Knowledge* storage. The moment *Knowledge* resets, the joy of Eternal Creation – *Truth*[36] – passes through. We experience this as laughter.
- Another is crying. Crying occurs when the reset involves *Memory* storage. As *Memory* resets the ~~Truth~~ within bleeds through and it manifests within you as crying.
- Any rapidly changing cognitive input tends to reset *Programming* (the eye exercise or listening to music[37] uses this).
- Sleep resets the mind on all levels.

This series will return to some of the concepts introduced in this eye exercise with later applications.

---

[36] Figure 4-4, back of book
[37] *Application 13*

Application #6A – Expanding Perception Through Space

With this tool you are extending your perception past your immediate spatial environment. In this application and the next in the series, you are to match your mind – a 'subjective event' -- to something around you – an 'objective event' -- that is not in your immediate temporal/spatial reference.

Exercise 6A -- Visualization exercise, "thinking is the best way to travel"

Sit yourself in a comfortable position alone, or with people. (In a class format, the author would have you listen to the sound of his voice as the author walked around you. He would have you look at something specific in front of you while he talked, and would ask you not to let your eyes stray.)

❑ Use your perception and imagine yourself behind the eyes. Then use your perception and imagination, slowly looking out and around the room, in a circle, without moving the eyes. Your eyes should still be looking in front and not moving. The images presented in this book are from the viewpoint of talking somebody through this exercise while in a condominium in San Jose, California.

Example: construct an image of the picture on the wall over to the left of you. What you would see if you were looking in that direction? Then move your perception around and imagine the other pictures. With your 'mind's eye', see the fan on the ceiling. Move your perception behind you and imagine the television and *VCR*. Keep it moving around to the curtain and imagine the open window behind you.

Using imagination, you can see the chair behind you and to the side, and the lamp next to it. Bring the perception around and imagine the sofa as if you were looking directly at it. Keep moving your perception until it starts coming back into your visual range. The idea is for you to make slowly a full circle sweep around the room, using perception and your imagination, <u>without moving your eyes or head</u>. Look around with the 'mind's eye', without moving the physical eyes. Use your imagination to <u>roughly</u> fill in the blanks. Recognize what is there around you and imagine it as if you were looking directly at it.

Avoid too much detail; form or shape is all that is needed. You can throw in some color or light if needed. The intention is for you to use the image to recognize and be aware of the actualities (that you cannot directly see) around you.

❑ Once you have established the horizontal plane that you first looked around, the next step is to jump up with your mind and leave that plane. With much of our perception or our awareness of the outside world, it appears that we are looking from behind the eyes and between the ears. The next step is you are to imagine that you are not there anymore (behind the eyes). Imagine now, you are looking from the reference of standing in that room; although, you are sitting.

Now, using this change in perceptional placement, make another circle around the room. This circle will be in a plane slightly above the first circle and your perception of the previous items will be slightly elevated, at a different angle. Therefore, this next step is to imagine what you would see if you were standing in the same room and just turning around. Again, your eyes and head are not moving.

❑ After you slowly go around once more, the next step is to imagine you-behind-the-eyes are up on the ceiling and looking down around you. Imagine you are on a stepladder and are looking down into the room. If you were doing it with the author, you would be looking down on both you and him, he would be talking and you would be sitting there. Look down behind you, make another mental circuit, and see what you saw twice before from a different perspective. Again, it can help if you imagine you were up on a ladder near the ceiling and looking around the room.

So now, slowly look around you (and down around you), as with the previous part, and make a full circle. This circle gives a different perspective, because of the altitude you have given yourself.

The general idea is for you to use your imagination to perceive something that you have not perceived in that way before (or not often). When the author was a kid, he stuck his head over a bed, lying on his back and looking upside down. He saw the whole room as being upside down. He imagined he could walk on the ceiling as if was the floor. While doing this he would imagine he was walking in the room with all the furniture in the room on the ceiling above him.

This exercise is similar. With this exercise, you are not physically moving yourself to see. You are just placing your awareness on the ceiling. Similar to the childhood playing, you are looking at everyday things from a different perspective.

❑ The next step is for you to imagine yourself passing through the roof until you are just past the roofline, outside the house. Imagine you are sitting on the peak of the roof. In class, the author would have you look with the x-ray vision of your imagination into the room; see him talking, and you sitting with a room of furniture around you. Now, you are to raise your perception and imagine the things below and around you. You can see in the next room. You can see up the stairs. You can see the front door. You can see the back door. You can see a neighbor's house. You can see in your neighbor's house. 'Color' it in with them watching *TV* if you hear the *TV*, or whatever.

Now, just as if you were sitting on the roof, you can look up and out and see the roofs of a multitude of other buildings around you. Make a horizontal circular sweep at that level, just as you did when you first started. You are to slowly moving your imaginary perception around. Imagine what you would see, if you were sitting on the roof. You know what is out there. You know there are other roofs. You know where the road is. You know there are cars out there. Make a general sweep of the area all the way around. As you are looking around, *slightly* 'color' in the details with your imagination. Do not let yourself be distracted by providing small details. The important thing is to recognize the actualities that are around you in your imagination; details are secondary to this application.

❏ Now you to use your imagination and move your awareness up into another horizontal plane. Now, imagine you are a mile up, looking down. Imagine what you would see if you were in an airplane or helicopter. Pictures of looking from this perspective are common these days.

You know that in that one little house below you in the colored patchwork pattern of rooftops and roads we are sitting and I am talking. Then there are all these houses next to us. If you look up, you can see the network of streets, the cars, the traffic, the lights, etc. As you start bringing your awareness up, you can look at the hills around you. You can start looking around and imagine seeing down the valley towards Gilroy, towards the south and southeast. Then move your awareness around towards the east and imagine you can see the valley, over the hills, across the way. Bring your awareness up and as you are moving from east towards the north, imagine you can see the hills starting to disappear in the distance and you see the beginning of the bay. Then bend your awareness back down the bay and look at downtown San Jose. Bring your awareness up and across, across the San Francisco Bay, and back around to the west until you start imagining seeing the hills again. See the ocean appearing behind the hills as your vista rotates. Be aware of all the other structures below you and all the cities below the hills.

The idea is for you to make a slow sweep with your awareness. Vaguely filling in the blanks using your own imagination with what you know to what you recognize is there.

❏ The next position is to imagine you are a hundred miles up. Now you can see the whole coast below you going from Mexico to Alaska and see the curvature of the earth. Perhaps remember some satellite photos and apply that perspective as you are doing this.

See the patterns of white clouds passing over the different blues of the ocean and the multitude of land hues. Accuracy is not that important. It is expanding your perception in these applications that is important.

You can keep on doing this exercise until you are 'standing' on the moon or 'standing' outside the solar system. You can keep on moving your visualization perspective out further and further. This exercise can increase your perception and helps open up your 'mind's eye'; it opens your mind's perception without using your physical eyes. This exercise can help open your Lens and Aperture of your *Perceptual Lens Array*.[38]

Where this exercise can take you, is totally limited by how much truth is in your mind already and your imagination.

The first example of this exercise expanded perception; we traveled up and out. And, you can go small. A suggestion is go out first and then bring yourself back in; and, just do not stop. It can become quite useful when coming back in to keep going. The first exercise went large and out; you can also go in and small.

Take an eraser on a pencil or your body. We are taught in school that there are a bunch of atoms set up in it so there is some kind of web or weave of material -- matrix. We are going to go smaller, and we are going to slip into the space between the weave of our body material with our imagination. We are going to go smaller and smaller so at first we can barely slip between cells, then the molecules. Now as we pass them and keep getting smaller we see the molecules are huge behind us.

We get smaller and smaller, and things become more blurry because they are much farther away. We can keep doing this and imagine ourselves in the vast amount of space between particles. Just as, we would find ourselves in a vast amount of interstellar space, if we went up and out.

This is the same application, just going in different directions. Instead of imagining going out, you go in. Either way, you are guiding your imagination by what is in your *Knowledge* and *Memory*. You are the driver – the operator. You are using the *Focus Control Buss* and your faith, applying your *Knowledge* without a direct physical interface (senses).[39]

You are matching a 'subjective event' – your mind's imagination – to an unseen 'objective event' – something in your environment.

---

[38] *I AM A I*, Chapter 4
[39] Figure 4-4, rear of book

This application consists of:
- ➤ **With the space exercises, inside and out, the assignment is to do three of each, preferably in a different location with each application. Vary where you physically are; do the exercises in different locals.**
- ➤ **Do each one for 5-10 minutes.**
- ➤ **Perhaps later, make an entry in a journal or workbook regarding where the exercise was done, distance, perceptions, and feelings afterward.**

Optional Space Applications:
- ➤ **From wherever you happen to be, while keeping the eyes still, explore your surroundings with your imagination. For example, if sitting at home, explore the house or apartment with your mind without turning your head. From your central perception point, place all the windows, floors, and walls around you and be aware of the furniture and other items. Increase your awareness in larger circles and be aware of things like the line of buildings across the street, in relation to you. Look around you with your 'mind's eye' and do not move your head. Do this for one minute once a day in different familiar settings for a week or longer.**
- ➤ **Look at the wall in front of you. Now imagine what you would see if that wall was not there. What would be the view from your current position? What would some of the items you would see? Imagine the buildings or vistas you would see if that wall, building, tree, mountain, person, etc. was not there?[40]**

---

[40] Thank you Superman comics.

Application #6B -- Expanding Perception Through Time

With this tool you are extending your perception past your immediate temporal environment. This exercise is similar to the previous one except it involves using imagination – visualization -- to extend your mind into time.

Exercise 6B -- Visualization exercise, that was the year that is yet to be

With this time exercise, it may be helpful to look at a corner of the room where two walls and a ceiling meet, or two walls and a floor meet. Pick a three dimensional space that is partially defined by some long-term physical object. If you are outside, look at something like a big old tree or a rock face. The idea is to pick something that is relatively solid, unmovable, and has been there for an extended period of time. Use your imagination to construct a small one-foot (20-30cm) cube next to it.

There are two ways to do this exercise. One is for you to be an observer of that cube from where you are sitting. Your perspective is that of looking at the cube and its surrounding environment.

Another is imagine yourself looking from the cube perspective to the cube's outside environment.

(Again, the imagery here is from doing this indoors in San Jose.)

❑　　As you imagine looking from or at that cube, move back in time to that which you know has occurred already. Start from this moment, and as you move back in time, watch us come in to the room. The light in that corner is going to change as the sun is moving across the sky, imagine this as you go back in time. Use your imagination to move the sun across the sky and it is moving the shadows in the room.

Do this and keep going back in time with your imagination, until it starts getting dark again as you are going from this morning and into last night. Envision seeing the cube as it was last night and dark, in a still empty room. Keep going until you get to before you went to bed. The cube is filled with lights from the lamps. Imagine the reflections of the lamps off the mirrored surface of the door blinds – vertical metallic blinds. Maybe a fly or bug crawls through the space.

If you were sitting in that upper corner, you can imagine last night and yourself or people watching *TV* below you. Use your perception and imagination and stay as an observer from that corner.

Observe the changing light of sunset in reverse, as the room gets brighter, and from that corner, watch the room and the day go back in time. From getting home from work and maybe walking below the cube, to coming from the bedroom and making coffee this morning. All are done in reverse below the cube, like a movie running backwards.

You can recognize many things as happening around or to that cube. You can do it from being an observer of the cube or seeing from the cube's perspective. You know air is, and has, moved through it. Once you get the alternation of light and dark, along with movement patterns down, with your imagination, start speeding up the cycles of the sun, going further back in time - days, weeks, years...

❏ In that corner, nothing much is happening right now because it is isolated and away from everything -- the one the author was looking at anyway (a wall/wall/ceiling corner). Use your mind and start speeding up the cycles of the sun, day and night. Visualize what you would see going back in time, periods of blurs of people with movement and no people.

Imagine that a number of bugs have gone through that cube; some cobwebs have come and gone. A lot of wind or air has gone through it, many reflections, a lot of light over a period of days, and numerous people have passed underneath while furniture has moved. Keep on going back and back until you get to the point to where this building is being built.

❏ Man defined that space we are looking at, by those three corners. Watch the building -- kind of like watching a movie backwards -- being disassembled around that space to where there is nothing but dirt below the cube. Go further back, and the area under the imaginary cube is a field, like the movie, _Time Machine_ based on the H. G. Wells book.

Where we were at it was a field and, prior to that, a plum orchard, and before that a bog. Imagine these vistas are happening below you as they go through their transitions. Recognize all kinds of flying 'critters' have passed through that cube.

❏ Now, keep on going back. Because the surface of the Earth is moving with the tectonic plates, the landmass we are on is moving westward (or toward the cube we are visualizing.) Eventually, if you go back far enough, you can visualize the land sinking and retreating from that cube until the cube is above the ocean. You can watch the continent retreat from the cube.

From the perspective of being in the cube, the space you occupy is staying the same as you watch the continent retreat across the ocean (as you are suspended above the ocean). Included with all this stuff are tons of bugs flying through (_Esp_ecially when you are in the grass or bog) tons of air, wind, rain, and storms. One can visualize all kinds of things that probably happened. Trees died in that cube, fell, and then new plants reoccupied the space. At one time, there was a beach below that cube.

This is where you -- the operator -- guide the visualization. You are actually creating this experience of guiding it for yourself and using imagination to roughly color in details and expanding your perception

44

through time. This to get you to recognize that many things happened in and/or around that cube other than what you see right now.

This exercise initially went backwards. We can go forward in time, also. This exercise will stay away from the concept of any apocalyptic change. It will work with how we recognize things to be now.

Be advised though; cities built on top of the rubble of other cities is an old theme. Usually in the past, the cities were razed and destroyed; then new cities built on top. Troy was like that. There was something like seven levels (maybe more) of the city of Troy. Crete is famous for that because they had so many bad earthquakes.

Cities were destroyed and they rebuilt the next city on top of the last one. Some devastation would occur -- economic, social, or ecological. Then the next city would be built on top of the last.

❑ Sit in that cube, and watch from its perspective all the people going through this room underneath the cube daily in the future. Several families have occupied the house, furniture is moved or changes, and you can imagine the building changes eventually until the building starts getting old and starts sagging. It will be torn down and then the cube is above the rubble. Then you can start to visualize someone building something else. There may be an I-beam going through that cube for a big office building or an apartment building, or it is sitting above a car parking lot. You can visualize that cube in a big chunk of concrete, farther along in the future. Could be a landing pad. The exercise's direction is dependent on your imagination. You know it will change and recognize <u>something else will happen</u>. Just avoid any preoccupation with details.

❑ Keep going further forward in time. Again, using the continent tectonic plate movement thing, imagine the hills to the east moving towards that cube as all those changes are happening below the cube. All this man-stuff has been built and has come down, built, come down, built and come down, as well as changes in vegetation, while the hills are growing higher and approaching that cube. Soon, that cube is going to be buried in the hills. You can visualize this, and set up this panorama of time in your own mind.

It is important to stress that when doing these imagination exercises, you should imagine or visualize as much perceived or recognized possible actualities as possible; using natural landmarks can help. Visualize the general picture - a whole picture. Do not let your mind stray off into the imagined details and try to make things up. Use your imagination to only lightly color in some of the details; just enough for you to recognize that objects or changes exist.

These time and space applications in this series can expand your perception. They can open up windows within your mind and more. They can give you a broader perspective on things. These imagination exercises use the *Perceptual Lens Array*, Cognition, *Knowledge*, *Memory*, Focus, and 'subjective event' feedback loop of your mortal mind.[41]

With this expanded perception, true choices can begin to become simpler and not so complicated - you see a bigger picture. Again, be aware of the existence of a myriad of details, and do not use the imagination to dwell on them. Use the imagination to sketch in only general forms and shapes for you to recognize.

It is very important for you to be the observer only. You are watching these things unfold, like a little child -- no judgments, because any judgment made will tend to cloud the exercise. Cultivate a 'disinterested-interest' in what you are doing.

I AM A I, Chapter 4 has shown how limited your perceptions are to begin with, and when you are judging something, you are constricting them further. In addition, given our perceptions are limited; most judgments made based on these perceptions will be in error because these judgments are made from incomplete data. In this case, they are judgments over something that does not exist except in your imagination.

Once you have learned both the time and space exercises, then you can put the two applications together and travel in time and space to jump around. You can leave the earth, looking down at it at any particular time.

For example, anchor yourself in the cube and anchor the cube in time and space. In the time it takes to snap the fingers, the earth is rapidly moving away from you in deep space (about 90 miles a second) and will not approach the cube for another year. Nor, will the cube show up on the planet in the same place it did before for many years. Just sit in the cube and watch the earth recede from you. In addition, watch the earth come around every year and recognize the multitude of changes that have occurred on it since its last passing.

The main idea behind these time and space applications is to get you to match a 'subjective event' - your mind's imagination, to an 'objective event' - something around you; to visualize something that you know is/was there; and, you can not immediately physically see.

---

[41] *I AM A I*, Chapter 4 or Figure 4-4, back of book

To do this exercise you:

➢ **With the time exercises, forward and back; the assignment is to do three of each, preferably in a different location with each application. For example, do the time exercise once while watching TV (during a commercial). Another time do it sitting in the yard, another time sitting in a restaurant, or at work. Vary where you physically are and do the exercises in different locals.**

➢ **Do each one for 5-10 minutes,**

➢ **Make an entry in the workbook or your journal regarding where the exercise was done, distance, perceptions, and feelings afterward.**

Optional Time Application:

➢ **As with the optional space exercise, pick a familiar place; somewhere you have spent some time. Imagine the surroundings you are in at a different time. For example, if on a bus during 'rush hour', imagine that you are on that bus (and what you would see) running over the same route it is traveling now but at 3 a.m. If in the living room at home, imagine the living room as it would look when everybody is asleep or gone away for the day's activities. The same can be done in a working environment.**

➢ **Do this for one minute once a day in various familiar settings for a week.**

Application #7A – The Two-sides of the Coin

This tool exposes you to your mind's perceptual lens makeup. The relationship to what you 'see' – perception -- and what you 'want' – desire -- is demonstrated in this application. The worksheet and a sample worksheet for this exercise are at the end of this series entry.

Exercise 7A – How do I see _____? Or, the mind and heart are one thing.

Your perceptions and your desires are one thing. A change of perception brings about a change in desires; a change in desires brings about a change in perception. This is very similar to the relationship between electric fields and magnetic fields.[42] Just as these changing fields make up one thing, *EMF* – (*Electro Magnetic Force*), so does your perceptions and desires constitute one thing.

An example of how one affects the other can be seen in the change from child to adult. Many things you wanted as a child you no longer want as an adult; simply because, you 'look' at things differently now.

This application exposes to you the relationship between your perceptions – what you 'see' (or do not see) -- and your desires – what you want (or not want).

Be advised that you can have perception without desire, but you can not have desire without perception. All desire is based on a perception of lack (or...lack of perception?). Even though that perception may not be clear, a perception of 'something else' is involved.

Again, (this cannot be repeated enough) the idea is to do this as a totally objective observation exercise and be careful about making any judgments/choices. Try to make none. Just watch yourself, as if you are looking at pieces while doing a jigsaw puzzle. "This piece is brown with a bit of green on it. This other piece is brown, but not the right shade. Oh, this piece over here is the right shade; and it fits."

This exercise begins as *Application 4* did. Look around the room and pick something, anything. Then, on the worksheet, write down what the object is and ask, "What do I see of _____?" Then, enter a short list of perceptions on the worksheet to answer the question. You can insert anything you want into the blank. Start with simple everyday items like the table, the wall, this finger, frying pan, etc. -- any subject is applicable. Fans are used as examples.

In fact, it is relatively important, when you pick something, to not to be exclusive; just like the truth perception exercise (*#4* in the series). And, like

---

[42] A change in an electric field creates a changing magnetic field; a change in a magnetic field creates a changing electric field. *I AM A I*, Chapter 3

that exercise; remember to give it the *K.I.S.S.* (**K**eep **I**t **S**imple **S**tupid). (Do not try to solve or 'see' everything.)

After doing this with simple objects first, you can expand this application in to life, God, the world as a whole, your culture or society, other people, mate, boss, friend, etc.

Once you have made a short list of perceptions on the worksheet – what you see, go through the perceptions on the list and ask the question: "What *do I 'want' from the perception of* _____?" That is the other half of the same question. *"What do I see and what do I 'want' from what I 'see'?"* Your perceptions and desires are linked.[43]

An example of this application is "What do I see from this table and what do I want from this table?" Remember, <u>any subject is applicable</u>.

You may be tired when doing this exercise. You may see a table as a thing to rest on. What the want it to do is prop you up. There are other things besides that like: not collapse when used, hold food, to write on, etc. And, that is all you may see right at that one moment; to hold your head up. There are other things besides that; are there not? There may be many other things. You are to record the things you see about that item you picked and are seeing in that one block of time.

The purpose of this exercise is for you to explore yourself; so, making a list can be relatively informative. This list can be your objective reference and help you increase your understanding around the spectrum of your perceptions and desires that you will explore.

After you ask, "What do I see _____," and "what do I want from _____"; you ask, "what could there be that I do not see about _____?" So you can ask, "What could there be about this table that I do not see -- ~~see~~?"

An example is a knot in the wood of the table. Layers of the knot go through the table. You can see the rings of the knot. (And, there are rings in that knot that are imbedded in that table that you cannot see.) So, what is there about the table you do not see? You cannot see the fasteners holding the table together.

You may say, "I am using it to hold me up." What you do not see right now is your use of it to hold your food up, or you use it to hold a piece of paper while you're writing. Recognize there are aspects that you do not see.

If you saw a table as a thing to rest on and picked that one that was most important to you at that moment of time, this was your desire influencing your perception. What do you want from the table now?

---

[43] Every desire involves a set of perceptions, *I AM A I*, Chapter 4

That was what you wanted at that moment, for the table to hold you up. You saw other things, but you may have not actually focused on them, so that narrowed your vision. That would help illustrate how your perceptual lens works here. Your perceptions have a relationship to your desires.

This also shows how any subject is applicable. Honest answers will affect your lens focus-refocus, how you set up and program yourself. This relates to the programming aspects of Figure 4-4 (back of book) and Chart 4-4;[44] which, in turn, controls the perceptions and desires through the focus control.

After you have made a list of what you see and ~~see~~ along with what you want, then add to the list what you do not want – ~~want~~ – from what you see or ~~see~~.

Observation and inquiry are your <u>only</u> jobs in this application. The idea is to show you how your perceptions and desires lead to how you are your programming your storages. For this to work, the only thing you need to do is to be honest and question. You have to be honest. Do not try to be too smart and fool yourself. Just be an observer. "I don't know right now" is an excellent answer.

Because when these questions extended into a very large subject like God, life, the world or that which is at the very core of your being, of course you do not know; and you may have to 'chew' on them.

Again, no judgment/choice. Because with judgment, your own ignorance can lead you astray. Judgment plus is the same as judgment minus. Either way, plus or minus, the flow is going to go through the Judgment triangle of Figure 4-4.

"This is a good idea"; can be just as detrimental as judgments against. The more judgment (what you allow to recycle through your lens) the more things will pump through your perceptual choice mechanism, which then will affect your choice, which will affect your programming, etc., and it will go into a loop again.

An intention of this and later applications is to help you reduce or recognize some of the loops that sustains or can contain ~~truth~~ (~~T~~)[45] within you.

To review this exercise, pick anything in the room or around you, like the truth exercise. Just pick anything in the room and write down the subject on the worksheet. You can use anything that comes to your mind. Using what is immediately around you, makes it easier, generally speaking.

---

[44] *I AM A I*, Chapter 4
[45] *I AM A I*, Chapters 4 and 5

Each item is going to have a dedicated sheet of paper -- worksheet. Put one category-item at the top of each worksheet. Any item will do, it does not make any difference. An example used in this writing is a ceiling fan (the sample sheet uses a table fan).

What do you see of this fan? Some answers might be:

- I see a hub with four blades.
- I see these blades in rotation.
- I see this assembly suspended a distance from the ceiling (or floor).
- I feel it is cooling.
- Etc.

Start making a list on the left-hand side of the worksheet of what you see in the fan. The next step, after you have written what you do see, in the other column, start writing what you do not see -- ~~see~~. Like, you do not see the electricity. You do not see the magnetic fields.

With this list of what you see of the fan and what you do not see, then you start asking, "What do I want?" from each entry. Some of these can be nothing/zero right now. A partial list may be:

- I want to know what the laws of motion are that governs it. That is a 'want' around a 'see'.
- You want the wind.
- You want the coolness.

You may think wind or coolness are things that you do not see. That may not be entirely true. If physically feeling is something that is regarded as perception -- sight, touch, feel, smell, or hearing, these are all perceptions.

The idea is to work with perception here. You may not hear the sound or the electricity, or may not have any 'wants' about them. You may want to include the electricity with any appliance and yet have no immediate desires. And, you may not want to be 'zapped' by the electricity – a '~~want~~',

Like the concept of rotary, there may be no immediate wants. And, if the fan does not go around, it has not any effect, so you may have a 'want' about that. Or, you do not want to know what that rotary action would do if you stuck your hand there – a '~~want~~',

The idea of this exercise is for you to see the connections between what you 'see' and what you 'want' – perception/desire sets. That is the primary purpose of this application. The idea is to have you see that these connections exist within you and how your motivation is directly connected to what you want/~~want~~ from what you 'see'/'~~see~~'.

After you have done this exercise several times, you may want to apply it towards a broader subject. *Life* may be one, another one *God/Divine*, *people*, or you can pick *the world*.

To do this exercise:

➢ **The assignment for this exercise is to do this seven times. Use the included worksheet.**

➢ **Make a list of what you see about the items you pick; what you do not see about them**

➢ **Write done what you want or ~~want~~ pertaining to what you see and ~~see~~.**

➢ **Do the same exercise once with a large concept like: Life, the world, God, yourself...**

➢ **An extra assignment that will expand this exercise is to ask questions such as, "Where do I think I am?" or "When do I think I am?" and answering with the previous Space/Time Imagination applications.**

OBJECT: table fan

SEE

Fan case		body		(barely see) moving blades		electricity		Moving air		People who made the fan	
WANT	~~WANT~~	WANT	~~WANT~~	WANT	~~WANT~~	WANT	~~WANT~~	WANT	~~WANT~~	WANT	~~WANT~~
There to protect	To collect dust	Look good	To collect dust	Move air when needed	more air when not needed	There to operate fan	To be shocked	The air to cool	The air to be warm	Do a good job of construction	To be exploited
	To rattle (vibration)	To be silent	To fall apart	To be quiet	Be dirty		Cause a fire	Feel the moving air to cool			
		Ozzle noise			Cause injury if too close body my						
		Made of several materials			Hit anything that air						

Assignment 7A Worksheet (sample)

53

OBJECT | **SEE** | **SEE**

| WANT | ~~WANT~~ | WANT | ~~WANT~~ | WANT | ~~WANT~~ | WANT | ~~WANT~~ | WANT | ~~WANT~~ | WANT | ~~WANT~~ |

Exercise 7A Worksheet

54

Application #7B –Before, During, and After

This tool involves preparation of your mental environment for an effective operation and introduces an observation exercise. You are to preset your intention and to observe your current state of being before and after an operation. This operation is an integral part of *Applications 8-10* and *13*.

Exercise 7B – Preparation of the 0perator

Your mind and heart -- *Perception/Desire Lens* -- is one thing; they are the 'flip' sides of the same 'coin'. Because the paradigm used by this book uses this concept, later exercises in this book call for a pre-setting of your *Perception/Desire Lens* – your mortal mind.

Before doing any exercises or applications for later elements in this series, a motivational examination, setting priorities, or pre-forming intention is part of the exercise and is called for.

In terms of your mind being the 'laboratory' concept introduced in *Application 1*, you will be setting up specific laboratory conditions for a successful experiment.

For some of these future exercises to be more effective, desires and attachments must be kept to a low number (your *Perceptual Lens Array*[46] cleaned up). Many schools of thought stress no attachments to the outcome of any exercise/discipline. If attachments are *0*, the denominator of the Truth/~~Truth~~ expression will automatically be *1*.[47] This would increase the likelihood of a successful application.

Some examples of pre-forming your intention may be:

❖ To ask yourself what is it you want from doing this particular operation.

❖ Perform a simple examination and begin with a stretch of your perceptions, make them as broad or inclusive as possible. See as much as possible with your mind.[48] Then observe what you want, from what you see. Remember to just observe, be aware that desires exist. (Recognize all these exercises are aimed at expanding your awareness and can increase the perceptions of your 'mind's eye'.)

❖ <u>Use your recognition of your own ignorance to generate a non-attachment to the outcome of any application before you do that application</u>. This, in turn, can help increase the effectiveness of any future exercise you do.

---

[46] *I AM A I*, Chapter 4, Figure 4-4

[47] *I AM A I*, Chapter 5, Formula of Effectiveness

[48] Or, perhaps do a short version of *Application 5*, Eye Exercise to reset the mind

With this expanded perception, be aware there are things you cannot see. Use this awareness of ignorance to foster a non-attachment to the outcome of the exercise. There are many things mental exercises can open up for you. Most of these things may be outside your perceptual grasp right now.

❖   For series entries *8-10* and *13*, you will be setting aside a 'block of time' to do these applications. You will be asked to use this setting aside a 'block of time' idea. You are to recognize that for that particular 'block of time' you 'want' – intend -- only to do this application (whatever the exercise may be). When you drift, remember your original intention – want -- for that specific time period. You are to use your preset desire – your intention -- to bring yourself back to the current application.

Many traditional meditations use a string of beads like a rosary or a mala. These are tools for setting aside a specific time window. Each performance of an operation is a bead. You do an operation, a word or sets of words, for a set round of the beads. This is the same concept as setting aside a 'block of time'. One 'round of the beads' serves as the allotted period.

❖   This application in this series also includes that before doing an operation and after doing an operation you are to observe the condition you are in. That is; notice how you feel before doing an operation, and then, notice how you feel after performing the operation.

One purpose of doing this with the latter set of applications entries is for you to observe the effects that these applications can produce in you. With many of the remaining exercises, you will be asked to observe these changes that the application has caused in you. This concept has already been introduced with earlier applications.

This exercise requires a time period of observation before and after an application operation. These time periods are part of those future applications. They are there for you to perceive effects and to preset your mind.

The way you are asked to approach this is:

❑   **Before doing an exercise** -- Just sit and notice how you feel: physically, mentally, and emotionally. What does your body feel like? What are your emotions right now? Notice the flavor of the thoughts you have been entertaining before the exercise. And -- this is very important -- establish your priorities for this coming time window – set your intention.

❑   **After doing each exercise** -- Again, notice how you feel. What does your body feel like? What are your emotions right now? Notice the flavor of the thoughts (if any) you have afterward. Sit with (and notice) how you feel – physically, mentally, emotionally -- after doing each exercise. This other block of time is to observe how you feel after doing the exercise – the effects. Again, observe your current state. Just observe, for about 2-5 minutes.

This application consists of:
- ➢ **You are to set your priorities or intention before doing an application and notice your physical, mental, and emotional conditions.**
- ➢ **You are to add on extra time before and after an operation to observe the changes the application produced in you.**

These two operations (pre-forming intentions/attachments and observation of current state) are an integral <u>part</u> of many of the following exercise applications in this series and are to be performed before and after doing each operation.

If you want, enter these perceptions and/or changes into a notebook or journal for future reference.

Application #8 – Meditation 101

The core concept to all meditations is introduced with this breathing tool. This application consists of an exposure to basic meditation using breathing exercises.

Introduction to meditation mechanics and breathing

All meditation can be reduced to a single concept, *a one-point focus on an event*. It can be an internal event, which is the common perception of meditation. It can involve an external event, like a candle or drawing. Or, meditation can involve both, like some athletics, dance, or martial arts. With the case of both, the meditation may be a one-point focus on the interaction between an internal and an external event.

The artwork of *Application 3* -- **Artwork, getting artsy-fartsy** -- serves as an introduction to this one-point focus concept. When doing artwork, one's focus can be, at times, only on the tip of the pencil, brush, or pen and the effect it is having on the paper. This is a one-point focus on an event. All meditations can be expressed as a variation of this theme. In the case of internal events, the focus may be on no event; and...this is still an event.

In addition, meditation periods involve a one-point focus over a specific period of time $f(\Delta t)$. The consciousness change that occurs with doing meditations (let us say y) involves a direct relationship with Δt – change of time. The greater Δt is the more it will affect y. As $\Delta t \Uparrow \Rightarrow y \Uparrow.$[49]

An excellent example of this relationship is how one feels getting out of a car after just finishing some long distance driving; the 'buzzed' disconnected feeling you get. In this example, the one-point focus involves a constant return to a form of mental peripheral vision. In addition, there are elements of the eye exercise of *Application 5* in the driving operation.

The effect on you is a consciousness change; you are 'buzzed'.
******************** ☯ ********************

Exercise 8 -- Breathing exercises, a navel operation

There are many methods of doing breathing exercises. There is a complete yoga[50] around breathing exercises (Pranayama Yoga). One of the reasons breath is covered first is that in later series entries, when mantras and other exercises are introduced, some of them can be done in conjunction with your breath.

In addition, these breathing exercises introduce to you the consciousness changes that can occur with breathing. This, in turn, can help with the accurate perception of effects of mental exercises you are doing afterwards – *Application 7B*.

Being aware of the effect breath has on you, can help you see what elements of the effects of an operation are due to breath and what elements are due to the mental exercise. At the same time, with this application, you also learn to breathe into whatever you are feeling.

All meditations involve a one-point focus on an event. Breathing exercises are an excellent introduction to meditation -- focusing on an

---

[49] *I AM A I*, Chapter 5, Formula of Effectiveness
[50] Yoga means 'union'. Yogas are approaches to union with the Divine.

'event' -- breath. Your one-point focus is on your body movement, feeling the air movement, the sound, etc.

Of the many methods of working with breath, this book will focus primarily on three basic methods. (All these methods are breathing through the nose only, and not through the mouth.)

When doing these exercises, your attitude or focus is to be watching and waiting. Watch your body move. Hear and feel the air moving through you. No thought is appropriate or desired. Watch and wait.

Wait until the allotted time period is over with. Accept no thought or make no judgment. Just watch your breath and wait. When you are finished with the breathing exercises, you then enter a reflection period; you are to extend your watching and waiting period an extra few minutes – *Application 7B*.

To begin this exercise, make your self comfortable, but not comfortable enough to fall asleep. Sit upright in a chair, sit cross-legged, lie down with your hands behind your head, or any position that allows you to be only partially relaxed. (Any position that is difficult for you to fall fully asleep in.)

The three different exercise applications you will be doing are:

❑ **Upper abdomen** → To learn this exercise, place your right hand on your chest and your left hand on your lower belly. This first exercise uses only your chest, and of course, the diaphragm. The only thing moving when you breathe is your chest and the top part of your shoulders – your right hand. Slowly breathe deeply in through your nose. Feel the air flowing into the upper part of your abdomen. Perhaps, pulling you shoulders back to increase the intake. Then, slowly exhale through your nose. Only your right hand should be moving in and out. Your left hand should not be moving. The only thing moving is your chest and upper torso, while your stomach is not moving whatsoever. Exaggerate the body movement if you wish. Your one-point focus over a period of time ($f\Delta t$) is the air moving through you.

❑ **Lower abdomen** → The second exercise is just the opposite. You do not move your chest or your shoulders at all, and just breathe in slowly, deep from the pit of your abdomen. With this breathing version, only your stomach and the lower part of your abdomen are moving. Only your left hand should be moving in and out. Your right hand should not be moving. Make an effort not to move anything else. You may have to exaggerate your stomach movement and maybe rotate your pelvis so you can do this. Notice how it feels as this exercise pulls air deep into the bottom of your lungs. Again, your one-point focus over a period of time ($f\Delta t$) for this application is the air moving through you.

❑   **Both** → The third method is a combination of the previous two done in sequence. It is done like this. When you inhale, you <u>slowly</u> and deeply inhale with the stomach; only your left hand is moving at first. As you get close to the end of the inhale, you expand your shoulders and chest with air, bringing the air to the top of the chest, your right hand begins to move after the left hand is almost done. Then, begin exhaling from your stomach, your left hand goes in first. As the breath finishes, you exhale with your shoulders and chest collapsing. Again, your right hand begins to move after the left hand is almost done. It is as if you are filling your lungs up from the very bottom first and expanding your body all the way up to the top. Then when you exhale, you are squeezing it out from the bottom first and, finally, you squeeze the top.

You may get dizzy after doing these exercises for a few minutes. These are altered states of consciousness. When you couple this altered consciousness from your breath with some of the other mental exercises, it is possible to get effects that are very interesting.
One of the goals of these breathing exercises is to get you to learn to maintain focus through consciousness changes ($f\Delta t$) by watching your breath. Breathe into what you are feeling. Just remember to breathe through your nose slowly to avoid hyperventilation.

As mentioned in *Application 7B*, when doing this application (and applications *9* and *10*), set a specified block of time aside to perform the operation. Use some objective time reference, like a cooking timer, a clock, a makeshift sundial, mala with one bead/breath, etc. This can help you maintain focus. This clarifies your intention and creates a specific window for that intention.
Your focus over this time period -- ($f\Delta t$) -- is only on breathing for a specific block of time. Feel the air going in and out of your body. With no thought, the idea is to just wait and observe. Watch the air movement and yourself.
And…if you drift, remember your original intention; what are you doing this for; and gently bring your awareness back to doing the exercise. Remember your pre-formed intention.[51]

In terms of the mind's mechanics,[52] these breathing and latter meditation exercises deal predominately with the *Perceptual Lens Array*

---

[51] Like, "I am going to focus on doing this breathing exercise only, for the next 10 minutes."
[52] *I AM A I*, Chapters 4 and 5

and the *Focus Control Buss* and somewhat limit the amount of ~~truth~~ that goes through choice in the matrix of Figure 4-4 [temporarily reducing ~~truth~~ chosen ($\mathcal{T}_C$), ~~truth~~ perceived ($\mathcal{T}_P$), and total desires (D_S)[53]]. It does this by preoccupying the mind with an internal event -- breath.

At the same time, this application involves a manipulation somewhat of the 'subjective event' loop in your matrix. This exercise can also help you to foster an awareness of your body as well.

This series entry consists of:

➢ *Get into a comfortable position.*
➢ *Do a pre-form of your intention and/or establish your priorities, notice how you feel at that moment, and cultivate a 'disinterested-interest' in what you are about to do – Application 7B.*
➢ *When doing these exercises, do a breathing method for an allotted period of time (10-15 minutes for example), and then stop.*
➢ *Sit for 2-5 minutes after each period of breathing. Notice how you feel. No judgments; just kind of childlike; notice how you feel – Application 7B. Observe. This part of the assignment and it is for you to just sit and feel what changes -- if any -- have occurred inside you.*
➢ *Perhaps enter perceptions or feelings into your workbook or journal.*
➢ *Do each breathing method three separate times (this makes for 9 total sessions). If doing a number of these exercises in one sitting, allow a period of 15 minutes between different exercises. (just so you can see the difference in application effects)*

As mentioned previously, these breathing exercises can be applied with other applications. Once you as an individual get this breathing down, you can do breathing while putting your focus somewhere else. (Breathing patterns can even go into an automatic mode, where no effort is made to sustain that breathing pattern.)

In some of your future personal applications, you may be using the breathing in conjunction with focusing on something other than breath (one-point focus on a 'subjective event' in conjunction with an 'objective event' – air movement).

You can see that this exercise is an excellent introduction to meditation. In addition, this application introduces to you breathing into what ever is happening to you or what you are feeling at that time.

---

[53] *I AM A I*, Chapter 5 Formula of Effectiveness

Application [#]9A – Going In

This is an internal meditation tool using a mantra. This application exposes you to a one-point focus of using a word vehicle to drop inward.

An introduction to chanting and *Application 9A,*

As mentioned in the previous series entry, *all meditation involves a one-point focus on an event.* With mantras, the application of the one-point mental focus -- $(f\Delta t)$ -- is you focusing on a word, and you are using the words for a vehicle to the exclusion of everything else. More specifically the one-point focus is on the word and nothing else.

When you use a mantra, you are altering the flows through your *Perceptual Lens Array.*[54] Your one-point focus over a period of time $(f\Delta t)$ will be one perception – the words or the perception related to the words. An effect of this narrow focus is ~~truth~~ perceived $(\mathcal{T}_P)$ and ~~truth~~ chosen $(\mathcal{T}_C)$ will have a reduced participation within your mind/matrix.[55]

Any word or set of words can be used as a mantra. What mantra syllables – words -- you do use can reflect your perceptions and motivations though. One of the author's college instructors taught meditation and biofeedback.[56] He said, you can use any word for a mantra, and he is right -- you can use any word whatsoever for one-point

---

[54] *I AM A I*, Chapter 4
[55] *I AM A I*, Chapter 5, Formula of Effectiveness
[56] When not teaching, he was doing biofeedback research for the Naval Postgraduate School in Monterey, CA

focus. He used the word hamburger. His mantra was, "Hamburger, hamburger, hamburger, etc."

However, what word/s you choose may reflect in the change of consciousness because your previous perceptions and desires influence it – your associations with the words.

Be advised; this idea of saying a word (or set of words) repeatedly and relatively quickly in your mind for a specific block of time is the core concept to Transcendental Meditation -- TM.

Different mantra exercises (and even different applications of the same mantra) can produce different results -- changes of consciousness. When varying these mantras (and their applications), the different desire/perceptions involved can also produce varied changes within you. This is because your desire/perceptions focus is in separate areas.

Meaning, the change of consciousness feels different with this mantra than it does with that mantra, and different with this other one.

That is an intention of this series set – *Application 9* -- of exercises; these applications are to give you at least three different mantra chant forms, to introduce to you three variations of change of consciousness.

Application 7B consists of an operation where before you start some kind of chant or mantra session, or any other exercise, ask, "What am I doing this for?" Recognize what you want; pre-form your intention; set your priorities, etc. "I am only going to do _____ for this period of time."

Question your current paradigm, programming, perceptions, or recognize your ignorance; "What am I seeing? What do I want from what I see? I want to know what happens when I do this."

(For any new paradigm or perception to be taught, the old paradigms or perceptions are usually called into question.)

As stated previously, some of the goals, reasons, and/or desires for doing these exercises are: God, union with the universe or Divine, love, kindness, harmony within yourself or with the world, truth, understanding, knowledge, or just curiosity and experimenting. "What happens when I do this?" Just doing this to observe your own mechanisms is a very valid motivation – recognize your ignorance. "I'm doing this to know me, to figure out how I work."

Any intention that revolves around the concept of 'One' or recognition of ignorance is no problem. It is clear sailing, pretty much.

Exercise 9A -- Passive chanting, (Saying it in the stillness)

This first mantra to be introduced in this series is one many people know -- *OM*. It can be pronounced long ō and with m or it can be pronounced as *Aum*. This chant is conjoined with breathing, one *OM* per breath. You may want to say it aloud at first in order to learn it.

Inhale through the nose; then, exhale and as you exhale say, "*Aaauuummmmmmmmmmm*". (or *Ooooommmmmmmm*). The vowel part, '*aaauuu*' or *ōōō*, is relatively short in this application. The last part, '*mmmmmmmm*', is long and let yourself vibrate to it. Let yourself vibrate or resonate to the '*mmmmm*' part. Learn to ride the "*mmmm…*" part into yourself. This is your one-point focus – the vibration.

One *OM* is stretched with each exhale of a breath. Then, take another deep breath and *Aaauuummmmmmmmmmm*.

There are three basic ways to chant *OM*.

- *Aloud* as mentioned in the above example (one *OM*/breath).
- Another way is to say it *softly* to yourself, the word gently coming out with your breath.
- The third is no vocal whatsoever, saying it *in silence*. Saying the word inside your mind (one *OM*/breath).

Generally speaking, the more pronounced consciousness changes occur when the *OM*s are done in stillness; there are no body applications splitting focus. However, you may have to learn to ride the vibration by saying it aloud first though.

Once you get the hang of riding the vibration concept, say *OM* in your mind to the silence, in the stillness of your being. As you are doing that one-point focus on *OM*, you turn your awareness and everything 90 degrees away from your thought/emotional sets, away from everything and jumping into yourself with this '*mmmmmm*' vibration/sound.

As presented earlier, the silent method can be the more powerful one. This is true for most mantras (with a few exceptions). A deeper trance can ensue when the body is not involved.

As with the other exercises, before you start this exercise, set a specific time window to do this exercise. You have the cooking timer (or beads, or whatever) out. Do this exercise for 20 minutes.

And…remember your original intention; you are going to do _____ application for a _____ time only. Remember that this is the only thing you are going to do. If you start drifting, remember: "I don't want to do that now, I want to do this." And go back to the exercise. Kind of like; a person on a roller coaster thinks, "I got to remember to write something down for the report. Oh, but I don't want to do that right now, I want to have fun and finish riding this." This is returning to your original intention.

Maintain your focus!!!   Growth comes from bringing yourself back. Momentarily remembering your immediate priorities for that time window can help.

There are a number of swimming and water analogies that can be made with meditation. One trick of doing an exercise can be similar to a swimming stroke. All swimming styles that are taught have two elements, a stroke and a glide. In some the glide is long like the breast or side stroke. Back stroke and crawl the glide is shorter while the butterfly has the glide almost non existent. The usually recommended action for a swimming style is stroke, glide; stroke, glide; stroke, and glide. This translates as work, rest; work, rest; work, rest...

With this exercise, the operators can do this inside themselves. The stroke can be in the inhale, or in the 'Ooo", or 'Aaauu' part, and the glide is in the 'mmmmm' part. You can learn to stroke and glide in your own head. Burst of focus, rest or glide, burst of focus, rest or glide, burst of focus, rest or glide, etc. Moving deep inside yourself. Stroke, focus, glide. Go back deeper. Stroke, glide.

Another option is letting go and entering your being serves as the glide. It is shutting everything down and riding the sound (or vibration), while empty.   The stroke in this instance is the inhale and the initial sounding 'Aaauu', the glide is the exhale and the vibrating 'mmmmm'.

Stroke-glide can be considered more active while dropping into yourself can be considered more passive. OM is one of the passive chants that is being introduced now; along with the stroke-glide aspect which, can be more relevant when we get into some active aspects of focus as with music.

The idea that is being presented here is that there is more than one way to do any one of these chants. One way is like swimming, while another is equivalent to floating in the water, exhaling, and sinking rather than stroking.[57]

And...no matter which way you do it, whenever you drift – start thinking, recognize it and re-evaluate or remember priorities. "What am I doing for this block of time?" Gently bring your focus – attention -- back to doing what you want to do, in this case, the exercise application.

Your growth begins when you catch yourself.

Remember, that if you just keep asking yourself that question when you drift ("What do I want to do right now"), this can help you stay focused. This idea of "remember what I am doing for this block of time" can be

---

[57] An exercise taught in swimming class that shows the student that as long as you have air in their lungs they will float.

applied to <u>anything</u>. It is prioritizing your actions in the moment. The process of doing this is elementary and involves the basic mechanics of refocusing your mind/matrix.

The exercise consists of:
> *Get into a comfortable position (but not too comfortable).*
> *Do a motivational analysis or establish your priorities or intention for the next block of time and cultivate a disinterested-interest in the exercise's outcome and notice how you feel – Application 7B.*
> *When doing these exercises, do an* **OM** *chant for an allotted period of time (twenty minutes for example), and then stop.*
> *The last part of the assignment is just to sit; after each period of chanting, sit with what you are feeling for 2-5 minutes. Notice how you feel. No judgments; just kind of childlike notice how you feel. Observe your body and state of being -- Application 7B.*
> *Do a chant method three separate times with each of the three methods – aloud, softly, and in the stillness -- (9 times total). If doing a number of these exercises in one sitting, allow a period of 15 minutes between exercises.*
> *Enter any thoughts or feelings into a workbook or journal if you wish.*

Voluntary and Optional Exercises
> *Do the above exercise using* I Am,[58] *'Iiaammmmmmmmmm'.*
> *Something else can be added onto this chant that can alter its effect. Take the* **OM**, *together with your breathing, and go through your mind and remember a musical chord that gives you 'goose bumps'. Some musical chord from some favorite song that gives you a goose bump reaction. Then you say that* **OM** *to yourself in that chord.* ♫**Aaauuummmmmmmmmmm**♫ *(breathe).* ♫**Aaauuummmmmmmmmmm**♫ *(breathe)...*

---

[58] Doing the above chant with the Name of the Nameless One; with the Name that the Nameless Desert God gave to Moses on the mountain.

Application #9B – Going Out

This is an external meditation tool using a mantra and an object. In this exercise, you are exposed to an application that is the opposite of the previous exercise. The one-point focus in this application is on something outside of you – *Application 3* yantra or mandala.

Exercise 9B -- Affirmation chanting, looking away

The second mantra to be introduced in series *9* is an affirmation exercise. An excellent example of an affirmation exercise that is already out in world religions is the Nichrin sho-sho Buddhists chant: *Nam-Myo-Ho-Renge-Kyo*. Affirmation chanting also appears in many shamanic practices. Affirmation chants are also called power chants. Nichrin sho-sho Buddhists claim whatever you chant *Nam-Myo-Ho-Renge-Kyo* for, you will get.

Essentially, *Nam-Myo-Ho-Renge-Kyo* means, "I will follow the chosen way to peace and enlightenment." At least, that was what the author was told by the people who taught it. Still, it is an affirmation/reaffirmation chant. An affirmation chant can be done with or without devotions. It is an affirmation of a direction you want to go in chant.

However, because *Nam-Myo-Ho-Renge-Kyo* happens to be a mouthful for non-Japanese speaking people, you may want to develop a chant that has meaning for you in your native language. Like:

- "I'm going to do this, I'm going to do this, I'm going to do this."…
- "I will _____.", "I will _____.", "I will _____.",…
- "I will follow the chosen way", "I will follow the chosen way.", "I will follow the chosen way."…

- "I will go to peace", "I will go to peace", "I will go to peace"…
- "I will go to God", "I will go to God", "I will go to God"…
- "I will be one with the Universe", "I will be one with the Universe", "I will be one with the Universe"…

When doing an affirmation chanting session, say a number of the chosen affirmation phrases per one breath. When you run out of breath, inhale. It is even possible to say one chant phrase while inhaling. With this chant, as with the others, you may develop a rhythm with breath. Affirmation exercises can be the exception to the 'say it in silence' rule mentioned in the previous exercise.

Recognize the "I" element, using breath, along with the choosing element in the chant, and expressing it physically produces the effect.

Again, you do several affirmations in one exhale and perhaps one affirmation with the inhale. Part of the physical effect of this chant on you will be due to breath.

When first doing this chant, do this exercise with eyes open, you are to have something for your eyes to converge on in order to have a one-point physical focus.[59] Your one-point focus over a period of time ($f\Delta t$) for this exercise is with the words and your focus will be on the mandala or yantra you made in *Application 3*.

This is only one of the ways the mandalas created in *Application 3* can be used. Your eyes are to stay on that yantra or mandala as your mind stays on the words. <u>No other thought is appropriate</u>. You should keep your eyes on the center of a mandala while saying something like:

- *"Nam-Myo-Ho-Renge-Kyo, Nam-Myo-Ho-Renge-Kyo, Nam-Myo-Ho-Renge-Kyo"*
- "I will do this. I will do this. I will do this. I will do this."
- "I choose peace. I choose peace. I choose peace. I choose peace."
- "I will follow the chosen way to _____. I will follow the chosen way to _____. I will follow the chosen way to _____.", etc.

It is strongly advised, for this exercise, that there is only one thing to look at and that 'something' does not move. It is also strongly recommended that whatever you are focusing on be in black and white.[60]

<u>*Do not let your eyes or your mind drift from that object while chanting.*</u>

---

[59] *Nam-Myo-Ho-Renge-Kyo* uses a gohonzon – a black and white calligraphy scroll.

[60] This way less information – no color – is coming into the mind from the outside.

There are a couple of advantages to doing it this way – to something specific; one is you are maintaining a physical focus as well as a mental one. Also, there are less visual distractions this way; it decreases 'objective event' perceptions that are present at Choice.[61]

You may want to experiment with different chants. Then, pick one you like to do constantly. And...just so you can see the difference in effect, you are also encouraged to try this type of chant with the eyes closed as well as open.

Again, doing this exercise exerts your focus over a change of time -- $f(\Delta t)$; it is exercising your 'focus muscle'.

This application can help strengthen your focus and resolve. All of these exercises do in the end. They are applications of the formula and the mortal mind matrix model.[62] The stronger your focus is, the more effective the chant is going to be.

Remember, in this chant as well as with almost all meditations no thought is appropriate while chanting except the chant.

In terms of the mental mechanics involved, this chant is tweaking aspects of the human mind/matrix (decreasing D_S, $\mathcal{F}_P$, and $\mathcal{F}_C$ while attempting to increase T_P and T_C).[63] An affirmation chant is playing with desire, perception, choice; desire, perception, choice; desire, perception, choice loop. The use of this exercise with constancy can affect your total *Programming* through the exercise of choice using repetition.[64]

This exercise is to:
➢ *Get into a comfortable position (again, not too comfortable). When doing the exercise with eyes open, hang the mandala/object on the wall at eye level and position yourself before it about 3-4 feet (1+ meter) away from it.*
➢ *Before each session, pre-form intention, cultivate a disinterested-interest, and establish your priorities -- Application 7B.*
➢ *Perform an opening ritual like bowing before the mandala/object three times, one mantra and one bow per breath. Emptying your mind, except for the words, as you do so.*
➢ *Do an affirmation chant for at least 20 minutes.*
➢ *When done, perform a closing ritual like; again, bowing before the mandala/object three times -- one mantra and one bow per breath.*

---

[61] *I AM A I*, Chapter 4 and Figure 4-4 in back of book
[62] ibid
[63] *I AM A I*, Chapter 5, Formula of Effectiveness
[64] Example: *I AM A I*, Chart 4-4, *H10*

Again, in emptiness. (The before and after bowing ritual clearly marks a beginning and a closure to this exercise.)

- ➤ *Do an affirmation chant session <u>aloud</u> at least three separate times.*
- ➤ *Do an affirmation chant session <u>softly</u> to yourself three separate times.*
- ➤ *With both ways, develop mantra rhythm with your breath. If the eyes are closed, focus behind the eyes, go all the way back in. With eyes open, focus the eyes on one specific thing (like the mandala) and <u>do not let the eyes drift.</u>*
- ➤ *Sit for 2-5 minutes after the chant session; in order to get a perspective on how it feels afterwards --* **Application 7B.**
- ➤ *Enter any thoughts or feelings into your notebook or journal.*
- ➤ *Do both methods – aloud and in silence -- with the <u>eyes open</u> looking only at the mandala or yantra three times. Then, do both methods with the <u>eyes closed</u> three times (making 12 separate chanting sessions).*

One of the purposes this specific type of exercise was chosen is it is an example of an active affirmation whereas *OM* is a passive and a dropping in. This exercise, instead of a dropping in, is going out and involves a participation in a specific perception/desire operation loop.

Application #9C – Inserting the Divine

This is a devotional meditation tool using a mantra. With this application, you are exposed to adding the concept of the Divine to an exercise and how this alters the operation.

Exercise 9C -- Devotional Chanting (May involve the G-word)

The third mantra category is devotional, also known as a heart chakra chant. There are all types of devotional chants in world religions -- the Psalms in Judaic and Christian traditions, Hari-Krishna from India; they are all devotional. The rosary is a devotional form of mantra.

To help you understand devotional chants, one reference involves a desire for union with something greater than yourself; all devotional chants involve a recognition of 'something' grander than you. The previous mantras and chants were more steering in, steering out, this way, that way. They are involved with dealing with mental operations – manipulating your mental direction. Previous meditation exercises can be done without any concept of a Divine Being -- God.

Throw in the concept of a Divine Being and now the chant turns up the drives, turns up the fire. You are working more with the fire aspect of the spiritual, the emotional, the desires.

As long as there is some sense of a Creator/Creatrix in an operation, it has a devotional element. There are so many directions and modalities that devotional can go. Devotional can carry in to Shamanism as well as Islam. Devotion is an element that is at the core of almost every religion. The concept -- recognition of something greater and the desire to be with or at-one with -- is used different ways. It is the same concept; just the individual – mortal -- perceptions and philosophies of what that One may be change.

Devotional may also involve a degree of contemplation of God's Glory.

Devotional mantras are also known as prayer vehicles. Psalms are prayer vehicles. <u>Prayer is a 'heart song' communion from the Created to the Creator.</u> The bible's psalms are very old 'heart songs' to God.

Some 'heart songs' have words and there are others that are wordless. Words give the 'song' a set structure; it can keep you from drifting.

With this devotional application in this toolkit, you are being introduced to the concept of the 'heart song' through a set of mantra/words. You can pick a devotional mantra already established in a world religion or you can develop your own 'heart song' to your perception of the Creator/ix, which may or may not have words.

The 'heart song' music begins in the heart and mind – your intention, not the voice or the words. The heart is singing, guided by your intention -- perception. The voice is only expressing what is in the heart.

One of the nice things about devotional mantras is that they tend to pre-form your intentions automatically.

With the previous mantras and chants, desire was kept at a low volume to little/no strong desires at all. *Applications 9A and 9B* mantras and chants kept desires singular and low volume, one perception – the chant -- and one desire – do the exercise. When you begin to perform devotional chants, you start turning up the volume of your desire a bit (along with, introducing numerous perceptions). This is the desire for the One (D_{Tp}), and it is made stronger, more specific, or cultivated.[65]

With this exercise, as with the previous ones, you are using words (or a series of perceptions) as vehicles; they are your one-point focus. You use these word vehicles as vectors for your one point focus.

This application, unlike the previous exercises, you are not only using words where the words do not mean anything, or have very simple meanings. Instead, you are including whole concepts involving perceptions/desires into the words. You are 'pumping' specific concepts through your mind.

You are turning up the volume on desires, and perceptions are increasing. And...you are still doing a one-point focus. For example, one simple devotional is a 'Glory Be'. *Glory be to the Father, Son, and Holy Spirit. Glory be to the Father, Son, and Holy Spirit*, etc.

The author, in teaching this, has found many people have trouble with popular Christianity and a Christian God, due to some bad experiences. Therefore, it is encouraged that you develop your own devotional mantra; something that is already established in a religion or something that fits with your perception of the Divine. Just saying "*Glory be*" can work.

One problem with most existing devotionals is they tend to be long, wordy, and there is a large amount of memory work with them. Like the Rosary beads, or the prayer of St. Francis, or any one of the Psalms. It is usually a long wordy thing. You know, "*Yeah, though I walk through the valley of death, I will fear no evil because God is with me, etc.*"[66]

Or with Hari Krishna which, is done as: "*Hari Krishna, Hari Krishna, Krishna, Krishna, Hari, Hari, Hari Rama, Hari Rama, Rama, Rama, Hari, Hari*". Most devotionals tend to be long and wordy.

---

[65] *I AM A I*, Chapter 5, Formula of Effectiveness
[66] 23rd Psalm

Whereas, you can also use a one word devotional like Amen -- "♪A...men, a...men, a...men, amen, amen...♫". This too can also be useful; and it is relatively easy to remember.

And...as mentioned, traditionally, most existing devotional chants do involve a lot of memory work or use a book as a tool.

Application 10B is an example of an exception to this.

Like the other mantras, this chant can be coordinated with breath. This mantra is to be done with the desire at medium or low volume within yourself. It is better to avoid a devotional at a high desire volume, because it can be somewhat counter-productive if perceptions are not 'one' or focused on the whole (of which, you are a part). (To be 'one', is to unify a number of perceptions into one perception; a perception that is comprehensive or non-exclusive.)

When perceptions start being skewed or divisive and the one desire starts getting at very high volume that is when the individual may start getting into fanaticism.

This is a condition where a person's perceptions tend to be divisive or exclusive (limiting truth perceived [T_P] and truth chosen [T_C]). When perceptions and desires are many and at high volume -- without any exercise of choice control – is a condition where the individual may also enter the psychotic realm. (Which, may not be that far from a being a fanatic.)

This exercise is:
- ➤ *You are to get into a comfortable position (but not too comfortable).*
- ➤ *Do a motivational analysis or establish priorities and intention for the next block of time, along with cultivating a disinterested-interest – Application 7B.*
- ➤ *The assignment is for you to use 'Glory Be', create your own, or find an existing devotional mantra (Hare Krishna, Lord's Prayer, a line from the Koran, rosary, Amen etc.).*
- ➤ *Do the chant for 20 minutes. (Or, if you are using beads like a rosary or mala, one round of the beads.)[67]*
- ➤ *Then, sit with what you are feeling afterwards for 2-5 minutes – Application 7B.*
- ➤ *Perhaps, enter how you feel in the workbook.*
- ➤ *Do this on three separate occasions.*

If you do any degree of experimenting, stay with one general action per sitting. Whatever application used, be constant through the whole

---

[67] Rosaries and malas – prayer beads – were the objective time reference used before there were clocks.

exercise. Meaning, do not change from chanting *OM* to *Nam-Myo-Ho-Renge-Kyo* in one sitting.

Additional note: those who have a problem with the Divine or Divine concepts can do a devotional with a reference toward the concept of Oneness, a Unity, the Universe, or the stars. You can also facilitate this exercise using a verse from a love song, any love song you want, as a mantra.[68] The important points of this exercise are: holistic motivation/intention and perception, the breath, the mantras, and everything is focus, focus, focus, focus....you drift, refocus...

Those of you who feel there may be a Divine and you do not know what this Divine is, good. Use this; use the sense within you that there may be *Something Else* and you do not know what that *Something Else* is.

Application #10A – A Non-action Action

This is a mantra-less silent meditation tool. This application is an extension of the previous exercises and involves the idea of having your one-point focus on an event being no 'subjective event' – no thought.

Exercise 10A -- Empty mind exercises, drawing a blank

Series *9* had you focus on a specific 'subjective event' with in your *Perceptional Lens Array*,[69] like a mantra. This particular exercise is to produce a one-point focus $f(\Delta t)$ on maintaining a no 'subjective event'

---

[68] St. John of the Cross used secular love songs and made them prayer songs towards the Divine.
[69] Figure 4-4, Mortal Mind Matrix, back of book

condition.

This application takes what you have been previously introduced to the next logical step. The exercise is in 'blankness'. No thoughts, zero, nothing, blank.

"null + 0 = hold that thought."

This essentially minimizes the 'objective' and/or 'subjective event' input of your mind/matrix. With this exercise, the choice is, "make no choice".[70]

At first, this idea may seem intimidating. Yet, there are many times in your life that you have had an empty mind and not recognized it. In athletics, this condition can occur in many different ways.

In fact, when doing some athletics, focus must be maintained to such an extent on an 'external event' such that, if you think, you usually 'mess up', or get injured. In this case, your perception becomes preoccupied – focus becomes split -- by a 'subjective event' at an 'objective event's' expense.

Many times, listening to or playing music can help one be devoid of thought -- *Application 13.*

In doing this exercise of a blank mind, you as the operator must recognize that <u>no thought is acceptable whatsoever</u>. This is an effort to shut down or step out of your subjective feedback loop. If you think of something you feel is important, set it aside and think of it later. "Not now, I'm going to do this exercise". And, bring yourself back to the exercise.

Momentarily, do your prioritizing – remember your immediate intention, then return to the exercise. Know what you want. All perceptions are approaching *0* in this exercise, and still there is a one-point desire for doing the exercise.

Again, perform *Application 7B* and set a specific time, a time with a beginning and an end to it with a timing device. This is a tool to help you return and not drifting while you are doing this.

In terms of mental mechanics, this is another application using a one-point focus with desire. The desire is, "There's only one thing I want to do for this period of time." You are bringing desires (D_S) to *1*, as perceptions (P_S) approach *0*. This will help facilitate the reduction of the participation of any ~~truth~~ with in your mind/matrix.

Everything should be empty or blank for this window of time. When you find yourself drifting, remember your purpose and correct. You are just

---

[70] No truth chosen (T_C) or ~~truth~~ chosen ($\cancel{T}_C$) minimizing choice total (C_S) -- *I AM A I*, Chapter 5, Formula of Effectiveness

sitting and waiting, empty. It is not as if you have to do anything, because there is nothing you have to do. You just wait; sit and wait until the time has passed and be empty. This can be done with the eyes open or the eyes closed.

With the eyes open, it can help if the eyes focus on only one thing. This narrows or simplifies the objective event. Again, that is where the mandala that was made in the third application can come in handy. Hang the mandala on the wall, sit in front of it, and focus on the center of the mandala, not letting the eyes or mind to drift. You can also use the flame of a candle, a blue sky, the ocean, the sand of an egg timer, etc. Just focus, wait, and be empty; no thought is appropriate.

(See *Optional Exercise* in this section)

This exercise consists of:
➤ **Because for the beginner it is hard to keep a blank mind indefinitely, the assignment is only for three to five minutes.[71] You are to get into a comfortable position.**
➤ **Do a motivational analysis – what is it you want, establish your priorities or intentions, and cultivate a disinterested-interest – Application 7B.**
➤ **Notice your 'state of mind' before the exercise.**
➤ **Do the blank mind exercise.**
➤ **When done, You are to sit and notice how you feel for 1-2 minutes (extending your watching and waiting time) – Application 7B again.**
➤ **Then afterwards, perhaps make an entry in the notebook or workbook.**
➤ **This is to be done on at least 5 separate occasions with the eyes closed and 5 separate occasions with the eyes open.**

********************* ******************

Toying with theme, tempo, and time
After attempting having an empty mind, you will find that it is hard to keep a blank mind indefinitely. It is difficult. Your limited finite temporal version of the Creation Matrix -- your mortal mind -- is constantly working, creating.

However, using exercises of mantras and music, you will find that the mind can be emptied with distinct short bursts for a relatively long time. When emptying the mind, there is the initial effort and then an effort to maintain the condition. What can be worked with is a continual repetition of the initial effort.

Instead of exerting an effort of maintaining a blank while waiting an

---
[71] If you wish to do this longer than five minutes, you are welcome to try.

extended period of time, it is *blank, blank, blank, blank*; and doing a series of 'blanks' while waiting. This exercise can have a similar effect to the exercise of moving the eyes very quickly. Mentally, this a similar operation of constantly changing cognition, but without the eyes.

Application 5 consisted of moving the eyes in such a manner that the eyes would rest on something only shortly. Then they would move to something else momentarily, then to something else, then to something else, etc. The eyes do not linger on any one thing. This was to be done for a specific window of time (one minute).

The movement of the eyes tends to blank the matrix automatically as the eyes and mind work together to establish focus and re-cognition. The *Eye Exercise* takes advantage of the brief moment that the mortal mind/matrix takes to focus to Cognition, and moves before the process is completed, restarting that operation with each movement of the eyes.

Instead of physically using the eyes as with *Application 5*, you use the distinct bursts of emptiness exercise and refocus cognition consciously with your mind -- blank, blank, and blank -- bypassing the eye mechanism, and doing it inside the head without using the eyes. This can be done in short bursts for a significant amount of time.

This 'quantum burst' type of approach can not only used with emptiness alone, it can be used in conjunction with music and mantras. Music is perfect for short periods of blankness -- blank, blank, and blank: an emptiness on each note.[72] You are not really thinking anything, just listening to the note. There is little or no 'subjective event'. With mantras, an emptiness can be injected with each word.

As with some of the other applications in this series, there is a direct relationship between length of time of emptiness – application -- to effectiveness.[73]

The longer you have a blank mind, the more significant the consciousness change. For effectiveness (if one element of effectiveness is measured as a change of consciousness), the change of consciousness will be directly proportional to how long the exercise is done over a change of time -- Δt. The expression Δt has a directly proportional relationship to consciousness/effectiveness; there is a direct relationship of change of time to change of consciousness.[74]

(The quality of the consciousness change will also be in direct relationship to how much Truth has been programmed in that mind/matrix – *Storages* – at the time of the exercise and your intention.)

---

[72] *Application 13*

[73] This can also apply to accumulative time as well, meaning repetition. That is; how many times you have performed that particular operation.

[74] *I AM A I*, Chapter 5, Formula of Effectiveness

The longer the operator has a blank mind, the 'heavier' their consciousness change is going to be.[75] This concept is not that complicated. As mentioned earlier, there are many different ways we have a blank mind and we do not know it. Athletics was used as an example; specifically, when you have to focus on a ball. If you think about what you are doing, you are going to 'blow it'.[76]

A significant part of the 'euphoria' of athletics can come from maintaining an empty one-point focus – having an empty mind for an extended period.

Your mortal mind/matrix is limited. With most things, the perceptual lens focus (your control of the array) cannot do two things at once. The mind's 'subjective event' must be empty or still to fully allow an 'objective event' to pass through it. If you are busy thinking, then you are not watching your physical situation. You can open up your focus to allow both events to occur, to come through the array (a form of mental peripheral vision). However, when it comes time to act, the focus must be on the event that is to be acted upon. With sports, it is usually an 'objective event'.

Driving a car is an excellent example of this. A detached awareness can occur where we are aware of traffic and the 'chatter' in our mind. Our mind's eye is open enough to 'see' both. When driving, awareness does not need that much attention, we listen to the chatter/thoughts. However, when the car needs our focus, the chatter and thoughts recede into the background.

Along with this, sometimes in driving a car, we create a long-term focus situations. The longer we do it; we get a consciousness change. As stated in a previous series entry, this is why our minds can be in an altered state after doing a long drive. You feel 'buzzed' when you stop driving from a long distance.

Another variable of this consciousness change is dependent on your motivation – intention -- when you focus or perform the application (what truth and ~~truth~~ are perceived [T_P & $\overline{T}_P$] and desires total [D_S] is in your mortal mind/matrix).[77]

To summarize, the major variables that influence your change of consciousness with an empty mind/matrix exercise are:

---

[75] To the limit of what your mind/matrix's current programming is capable of.

[76] An example of focus being split by 'subjective' and 'objective' inputs is *I AM A I*, Chart 4-4, *N2*

[77] *I AM A I*, Chapter 5, Formula of Effectiveness

- $f(\Delta t)$ focus over change of time…This includes long term as well as short term; how much you have done this exercise previously -- repetition.
- How much Truth that is already stored in your mind (*Knowledge, Programming*, and *Memory* specifically).
- Your intention – perceptions and desires – in doing the application.

This is a great exercise if you have to stand around and wait for something. Waiting. Blankness and empty. The author did this exercise a lot in the army. "Hurry up and wait", is the military credo. In waiting, the author would be empty and allow no thoughts to be entertained.

That is one of the interesting things about doing mental exercises in a crowd. No one has any idea what you are doing. True, you may appear a bit 'spacey'. And…doing mental exercises is a lot subtler than doing jumping jacks or hatha yoga in a crowd.

********************* ☯ *********************

Optional Application, Maintaining a physical focus <u>only</u>

This exercise simply involves sitting in front of a mandala or any object and not let your eyes leave the center of a mandala or object. This is a simple exercise in maintaining a physical focus only.

- ➤ **_Perform_ Application 7B**
- ➤ **Sit in front of the mandala or <u>any object</u> as in exercises 9B or 10A**
- ➤ **Do this exercise for twenty minutes, on at least three separate occasions.**
- ➤ **Sit and observe for 2-5 minutes afterward -- Application 7B.**
- ➤ **Enter any thoughts or feelings into a workbook or journal.**

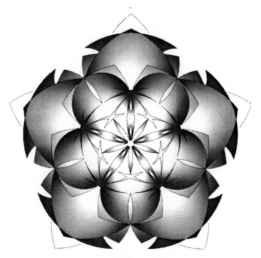

79

Application #10B – Riding the Divine

Previous meditation exercises are combined using a name of God in this tool. Prior applications are combined in other ways for you to experiment with.

Exercise 10B -- A possible combination, experimenting with the G-word

The next entry in this series to be covered is a combination of previous applications. It involves using a very short devotional mantra at a relatively high frequency, at heartbeat speed or twice your heartbeat (using your own internal rhythm) along with emptiness. Blank, blank, blank, blank, blank.

This application is very similar to using any word or mantra repetition introduced in *Application 9A*. The concept of constant repetition of a one word mantra is at the core of Transcendental Meditation (as was pointed out in an earlier application).

❑ The word or concept that your focus is on should be one syllable and very short such as: God, God, God, God, God... You can use the words Love, Jah, Allah, Mother, Daddy, etc.; any short word that connotes the Divine for you can be used. As you are doing this mantra, bring your attention or focus (*f∆t*) – focus over change of time -- inside, 90 degrees away from everything.

This is another exercise where the use of power/stroke and rest, stroke and rest, stroke and rest...may be applicable.[78] These rests however are for very short periods. The power or stroke part of it is focusing and saying the word 'God' the rest – emptiness -- is the short space between words. (God...God...God...God...)

Alternatively, you can also float, gently float back into it, and flutter into your being; riding the word repetition – empty -- with no rests.

Here again, because a God/Divine concept is involved, a devotional element is involved with this exercise.[79] If you have some love for the Divine, use the love that you may feel for God with it. If you do not know if there is a God or not, pick a word that you associate with the Divine Concept and say it in to your not knowing, "with the eyes of a child"..

You can use both mind bursts and love bursts as you do this mantra. The devotional element in this application is conjoined with another version of a continual mental mechanical preoccupation.

---

[78] *Application 9A*
[79] *Application 9C*

At first, try this application rapidly, twice your heartbeat. Later, on your own, you can do it at whatever speed you want. That speed is picked because it matches some of your internal rhythms. You may prefer to do it with each heartbeat. You as the individual may have to learn to experiment on your own and play in your head, with this, to see how it feels.

However, if you do any degree of experimenting, stay with one general action per sitting. Whatever application used, be constant through the whole exercise for that time window.

Experimenting

This exercise can also be applied to instrumental music as in a previous application.[80] Remember that as you are doing any of these mantras or exercises, you are just existing -- being. Your whole attitude is just sit and wait while doing them. Nothing for you to do but wait and do the chant/exercise.

Remember, an intention of introducing all these exercises are for you to explore yourself and to play with your mental mechanism. You can use these presented mantra exercise types in a multitude of applications. That was one of the goals of this series, to custom design your personal meditation approaches along some common principles – common mind mechanics.

Usually, mantras tend to involve you in relationship to some of your perceptions of the outside and yourself. And...it can go the opposite way, too ("null + 0 = hold that thought").[81] It is totally up to you which way you want to take it -- your intentions/motivations. When you are 'playing' with these ideas and concepts, recognize that there are different directions, vehicles or modalities, and ways you can take it.

No matter what you do: if you do anything over an extended period of time with one-point focus, there is going to be an effect -- consciousness change -- within you. You may not understand or even recognize this change. And...you do it to yourself. Doing mental exercises done in conjunction with regular breathing or deep breathing, this consciousness change can be augmented.

As with some of the previous exercises, with this and other meditations, you set a beginning time and an end time, set aside a time window.[82] With many meditations, something that automatically sounds is very useful like use of a clock or a cooking timer. See what time it is, and

---

[80] *Application 13*
[81] As in *Application 10A*
[82] *Application 7B*

wait until the clock rings the quarter, half, three-quarter, or the hour; or, do the exercise until the cooking timer 'dings'.

This objective time reference like a clock or timer keeps things clearer and cleaner for you. Use time. Although from the Eternal Divine's reference, time is non-sequitar. The Divine uses it to approach us – to those who experience time. You can use it as well.

> *"Okay, I'm doing this right now.*
> *"OOPS, I drifted. I forgot."*
> *"I've got to bring myself back."*

This time allocation can help keeps things clear for you. The time to stop is when the timer thing goes off. Afterwards, you can start thinking about some of the things that came into your mind while you were doing the exercise.

When doing the exercise though, <u>do not think about any thing</u>. You can always set the distracting thoughts on a shelf and say, "Later. I'll think about that one later."

For this application you:

- ➢ *You are to get into a comfortable position (but not too comfortable).*
- ➢ *Do a motivational analysis – what is it you want, establish priorities or intentions, and cultivate a 'disinterested-interest' in what you are about to do, perform Application 7B.*
- ➢ *Notice how you feel and how your mind feels before the application.*
- ➢ *You are to do three separate 20-minute Divine Name sessions. (at three separate times; meaning, several hours have occurred between applications)*
- ➢ *As with the other exercises, sit and observe yourself 2-5 minutes afterward, see Application 7B.*
- ➢ *Enter any thoughts or feelings into the workbook.*

Application #10C – Variations on a Theme

This tool presents numerous meditation options and variations. A number of previous applications are reassembled to introduce other exercise approaches.

Exercise 10C+ -- Zen and slipping between thoughts, options, options, options...

Up to this point in this series, the applications introduced have been playing with the perceptual lens related to what choices we make.[83] The previous meditation/mantra forms are manipulating the flows through the lens array – your mind. Your perceptions and your desires (motivations/intentions) are part of this manipulation along with the available choices. The idea of these applications is to make choices based on truths of the whole and unity, to reduce ~~truth~~ within your mind.

Applications using imagination, perception, and focus have been introduced. Imagination exercises today are called visualizations. Which are just other ways to play with the *Perceptual Lens Array.*[84]

Also, what has been touched upon in a previous applications is using the brief moment in time the *Perceptual Lens Array* takes to focus. The eye exercise was an example of doing that.[85] It constantly caused your mind matrix to refocus and in doing so, no or few choices (a decrease in ~~truth~~ chosen [$\mathcal{T}_c$][86]) are made, which directly affects your *Programming.*

---

[83] *I AM A I*, Chapter 4
[84] Figure 4-4, Mortal Mind Matrix, back of book
[85] *Application 5*
[86] *I AM A I*, Chapter 5, Formula of Effectiveness

"Now, for something completely different".

In previous elements in this series, it was brought to your attention that your mortal mind/matrix is limited. This makes stepping out of the mind a 'gilt edged' priority for anyone who is serious about metaphysical or spiritual studies.   In order to explore that which is beyond our normal perceptions we have to leave those perceptions behind.

All the meditations that have been covered, including the mantras, the breath, and everything that has been introduced; have passive and active elements in them, yet they are still dynamic in nature. They are doing something. Some are efforts in reducing ~~truth~~ (~~T~~) within the mind while others are efforts that increase truth (*T*) within the mortal mind/matrix. All the exercises up to this point in the book (except for the recognition exercise of truth, *Application 1A*) you, the operator, are doing something actively. The very act of meditation is an act. Even if it is to non-act, this is an act.

With most of the previous exercises, this action involves a manipulation of the mind/matrix operation. Previous meditation exercises used your mind's operation to alter what truth or ~~truth~~ it contains at any given moment. Essentially, you -- the operator, are setting a block of time to do 'something' within your head.

What if that block of time is set aside to do absolutely nothing? Instead of manipulating the mind/matrix, recognize the limits of the mind and 'step' outside those limits. This, in turn can reduce the participation of ~~truth~~ within the mind.

You are not your mortal mind. You are God's Creation. When you leave your mortal mind behind, the only thing left will be who you really are – God's Creation.

Option #1

This application is a truly passive form of meditation and was introduced as the watching waiting part of at the end of each exercise. An excellent image of this meditation is the Zen or the Taoist picture of a heron on a lake. A functional stillness occurs with the passive operation of watching and waiting – just being relaxed and paying attention.

St. Romuald[87] said, "Sit in your cell as if in paradise." You do not know there is a paradise around you (or in you for that matter), but there is. (The heron is probably more cued into the paradise aspect than any human is.)

This next exercise application is for your mind to be as a heron on the lake; watching and waiting in the whole paradise that is around you.

---

[87] Founder of the Camaldolese Order and lived to 150 years old.

This exercise is for you to cultivate a functional stillness or non-action arising from just being relaxed and paying attention. While paying attention, you are to be like the heron and watching your thoughts as the heron watches the fishes, without judgment or choice, and no action. You are watching your perception/desire or thought/emotion mechanism, which is reflected by the 'subjective events' that are created by your mortal mind/matrix.

Be an objective observer of these thoughts, daydreams, and fantasies. You are watching it all inside your head as if they are fishes. You are just watching your movie go by. And...as one thought passes by, another one arrives. The thoughts follow each other, and you are watching them from above. Like a bird, that already has had dinner. Be like the heron watching the fish below it.

Here is an analogy to fixing a record player. After the author got out of college, He started working in analog electronic repair places: TV and stereo repair, p.a. systems, alarms, etc. The first three jobs (the very first chore) the author got in these electronics repair stores would be they would give him a box full of parts; and say, "This is a record player; fix it."

The first couple of times, after putting it together though, the author would see the record player is not working properly. It was not doing what the author knew it is supposed to do. It is supposed to eject, it is supposed to play, etc. Because the author did not know what made a record player eject or play, the author would have to watch it go through the eject and reset cycles maybe 30 or 40 times. He would just sit and watch it, not doing anything except recognizing connections. He was just watching. (The author was being paid the same -- minimum wage.)

Finally, as the author observed, he saw 'this' connects to 'that', he saw that this notch goes there, and the wheel comes back. As said, the author may have had to do this at first -- watch it numerous times -- to digest what is happening with each part. Most of it was just watching, and finally in the watching; a cognitive jump occurs. "Oh, I got it! I see it now!"

Doing this inside -- watching yourself, watching the mechanism of the matrix inside yourself -- is a truly passive form. By not taking any active control anywhere here, you are using the focus/cognition mechanism of the mind/matrix on the mind/matrix itself, using the Cognition input only.[88] You are just watching with no judgments.

Watching your thoughts. Watching your reactions to thoughts. Watching what you are feeling. Watching how you are sitting. Watching the car go by. Watching your reaction to the car go by. The whole idea behind doing this is that certain reoccurring mechanisms will begin to

---

[88] *I AM A I*, Chart 4-4, *B5*

appear to you as you are doing this. Start watching yourself, looking at your mechanisms. This exercise addresses the old Oracle of Delphi adage, "Man, know thyself". This application is a beginning.

An excellent example of watching and waiting, in everyday life; is to watch yourself watching *TV*. Watch your reactions to watching *TV*. The *TV* itself is totally neutral. The reactions within you are what you have created through your previous mind programming to the *TV* programming.

The value of this exercise is that it exposes you to your parade of thoughts. Whatever meaning these thoughts have for you is what you give them.

Outside of you, these thoughts have no meaning. Once you cease giving these thoughts any meaning, you begin to step 'outside' of the mind's operation.

This exercise is for additional study. The exercise is for you to watch your thoughts. If you find yourself becoming involved with a thought-desire set, pull back and disengage. Remember why you are doing this -- your intention; even if, that intention is to fool around or explore your own head.

Breathing exercise can also help the operator relax into this exercise. Instead of watching the breath, you are watching your mind.

In this exercise, you are to:
> *As in the other forms of meditations, before you start this passive exercise, perform* **Application 7B**; *look at what are you doing this for. What do you want? What is your intention? How do you feel?*
> *Set aside three separate blocks of time (15 to 30 minutes) to watch your thoughts or reactions.*
> *Find a partially comfortable position.*
> *Watch your thoughts and wait.*
> *Enter some of your perceptions of the operation in to the workbook or your journal.*

You will find the chatter -- the mind/matrix chatter -- is endless. That was touched on in a preceding application. The human matrix, like a limited mortal mirror version of the Truth Matrix that it is, is constantly creating. One matrix is creating on a temporal level, and the other is working on an Eternal level. Most of the time, your mind's creations are meaningless chatter, based on what is in *Storage* – 'back of your mind'. They flit from one perception/desire set to another.

One of the things this application is addressing is for you to see this and just watch the parade of thoughts going by. To re-cognize it is there, that it exists, and to watch it. You will begin to see some reoccurring themes within them as you are doing this. In seeing these themes, a reevaluation may occur. In re-evaluating, perceptions, desires, and attachments may change; including, being attached to your own mind.

The next logical application of this is to learn to ignore your thoughts; ignore the chatter.

Again, this series entry is a passive application. The reasoning for these type of actions – learning to step out of your mentation -- are:

- Given: whatever meaning your thoughts have is what you give them.
- Given: whatever the thoughts say to you is going be limited by what is in your mind – programming – and are liable to be inaccurate representations – ~~true~~ – based on your limited perceptions.
- Given: truth is laws by which something 'works'.
- Given: the more you work in truth of an event, the more functional you will be in the event. And...conversely, the more you work with ~~truth~~ – not in the laws of an event, the more dysfunctional you will be in that event.
- Then: learning to ignore your thoughts can contribute to your increase function – effectiveness – in an event.

This exercise is more personal. Everybody has to learn to do this on your own. It is difficult to tell you how to watch and/or ignore your own thoughts. It is kind of telling you how to swim or walk.

Option #2

Another meditation modality that is used is called *Lexio Divino*.[89] An easy way to do this is to use the writings in a spiritual or meaningful book – something that impacts you. This application involves using a spiritual text, reading it, and sitting with it afterward.

Mechanically, this method temporarily (while reading) steps out of the free flowing thought-desire sets that come through the subjective input, to use mentation to get out of mentation (like mathematical operation of division by zero leaves mathematics).

Referring to the 'ringing' of the first exercise – *Application 1A*, it was mentioned that if Truth is perceived constantly, it could alter states of consciousness through this ringing.[90] The speaker/writer is 'weaving' truthful symbols, and the listener/reader is interpreting the symbols and resonating.

---

[89] A monastic Catholic exercise
[90] *I AM A I*, Chapters 1, 3, and 4

In that interpreting, the listener can make a mental 'jump' and leave the separate elements of the 'weave' and start to appreciate the 'cloth' of the subject matter. Kind of like seeing the <u>curved</u> sphere – a non-linear concept, that is implied by the <u>straight</u> lines of geodesic dome struts – linear concepts.[91]

A listener can leave mentation (their mental constructions) and enter the presence of Truth through mentation. The mortal mentation in itself is limited and temporal in nature.

In this application, the mind is intentionally preoccupied initially with some writings where something is being woven to imply that which is beyond (behind) the mortal mind -- an Eternal.

It is you, the listener/reader, which makes the dimensional jump in perception. A one-dimensional thread is woven to produce a two dimensional cloth.

This application involves a method of 'weaving thought forms', pumping truths through the mind. It does this with as much Absolutes as possible from your *Knowledge*, through the subjective event, via your *Perceptional Lens Array*, into Choice, thereby altering your *Programming*; and then, going around again.[92] Usually reading something that affects you, spiritually or inspirationally, can do this. This can start the ringing in the mind/matrix, *Especially* if the truths are augmented/increased each time it goes through the lens array.

The effectiveness of such an operation is contingent on the measure of truth already within your mind/matrix *Storage* to start with. A specific amount of truth applications must be present within your *Knowledge* for this to work effectively.

This application involves an intentional 'ringing' of *Application 1A*; and then, has you sit with what you are experiencing afterward.

This exercise is to:
➢ *Perform* **Application 7B.** *Establish what do you want? What is your intention? What attachments do you have on the results of the exercise?*
➢ *Pick a piece of spiritual writing that impacts you*
➢ *Read it*
➢ *Sit with how you feel, or sit with what that writing means to you for 15 minutes*
➢ *Do this on 3 separate occasions*
➢ *Write perceptions in the journal*

---

[91] Another case of a logic system – linear -- creates something outside of the logic system -- curved.

[92] Figure 4-4, Mortal Mind Matrix, back of book. Some examples are *I AM A I*, Chart 4-4, *I10-12* or *J10-11*

Option #3

There is another way to use mentation to leave mentation, still using the weaving cloth analogy. What if you are following some threads of thought or symbols within an idea weave, and all of a sudden, there is nothing there; a hole with nothing else to grab or to follow? A Zen koan can do this, "What is the sound of one hand clapping?"

OOPS. All of a sudden, there is nothing there. It causes the mind/matrix to refocus or reset. Every time it refocuses, there is still a hole that prevents full operation of the array, even to cognition.

In doing this, it is possible to slip between the threads of thought to enter another state of consciousness. A kind of slipping between the temporal thoughts and leaving temporal thought behind. As stated previously, because eternal and temporal are mutually exclusive, when an individual leaves the temporal, the only thing left is the Eternal one way or another.

An example or a spin-off of the koan idea was introduced at the end of *Application 5*. That is, when a series of unrelated cognized perceptions (with their subsequent reasoning and logic) are put in a semi-logical order to produce a new independent unrelated cognition.[93] This condition can cause the mind/matrix to completely reset. It is similar to pressing *Ctrl, Alt,* and *Delete* on the computer keyboard.

As stated in that application, when the mortal mind/matrix is resetting on the *Knowledge* level, an element of the eternal joy of God/Creation manifests in the matrix. We experience that moment as laughter.

Playing with these introduced exercises/mechanisms in this particular series entry are more of an auxiliary applications for you to experiment with. Everybody's mortal mind/matrix is programmed different.[94] Your applications will follow your intentions. This series entry is just putting it out there that there are a multitude of directions as well as approaches.

---

[93] As opposed to a series of unrelated cognized perceptions put in a semi-logical order -- there is no cognition, and the matrix refocuses, *I AM A I*, Chapter 4.

[94] Due to the choices they have made and the subsequent mind/matrix programming these choices have produced with their constituent perceptions.

Application #11 – *ESP* Cultivation

This tool introduces *ESP* theory. Basic theory behind all personal *ESP* events is presented; the mechanics of how *ESP* works within you and how you can work with it. There are no exercises in this entry of the series.

Exercises 11 -- Basic *ESP* theory, exorcizing the 'spooky'

The introduction to this *The Truth Tuning Toolkit* Exercise Series – *Application 1* -- stated there would be a minimum amount of theory in presenting these exercises. Because the exercises *11A* and *12A* are entering into intermediate applications of mental mechanics, some theory is necessary. This theory can help give you a 'from the top down' perspective (as opposed to seeing something 'from the bottom up'). The theory allows you to see connections or common points of reference.

Because the theory used in this book is so interwoven with other elements of *I AM A I*, it may be better to read Chapter 7, Concerning *ESP* Events and Psychic Phenomenon and Chapter 3, specifically, 3.7 - Time Ignor-ance.

This way this entry in the series stays 'relatively' short. Those chapters present these exercises and their theory in entirety.

Here is an example of some of the theory involved:

⇒   *There is only One Mind.*
        Postulate 2[95] states, "*God's Absolute Love has an Absolute, Logical,*

---

[95] Chapter 2, *I AM A I*

and Eternal Mind." There is only One Eternal Infinite Mind. Because this One Mind works with infinities within infinities within infinities...infinitely, the Logic of the One Mind works beyond <u>all</u> finite mind – mortal -- perceptual references.

⇒ *You have access to this One Mind because it is at the core of your very being – who you really are.*

The implications of *Theorem 13* -- (God's) *Will, Love, Logic, and Truth are One in an Eternal Creation* -- conjoined with *Postulate 6 -- I am God's Creation* -- is that you can never leave this One Mind for it is the very essence of your being.

⇒ *All ESP is through the One Loving Eternal Mind.*

Be advised that the following *ESP* exercises are a natural extension of the previous exercises – *Applications 8, 9,* and *10* -- because psychic perception (an *ESP* event) is a side effect of having an empty mind.

When you begin to step outside of your temporal (mortal) mind/matrix, the only thing left is the Eternal Truth Mind/Matrix within you; your given Natural Mind takes over. This is a metaphysical application of the *Right Angle Rule* (Chapter 3, *I AM A I*). To fill your finite/temporal mind – mortal mind – with non-temporal conveyed information, your mortal mind must be stilled. It is an indirect approach.

ESP involves and an internal communication within the One -- Eternal Infinite -- Mind. All *ESP* is through the One Mind. What that One Mind has access to, we all can access; because, the One Mind is the core of your being. This means that all the knowledge (and Creation capabilities) that is in God's Loving Mind/Matrix is available to you.

Since the Love's Eternal Mind is yours by the nature of God-Creation relationship -- you, *ESP* is working from the very core of your being. The major irony around *ESP* is being psychic is natural; it is not being psychic that is un-natural.

It has been said you are not your temporal matrix -- your mortal mind. You are not the mental/emotional sets that preoccupy the mortal mind. Your temporal mind is your vehicle in your temporal body. Just as your temporal body is your vehicle in temporal spatial creation – physical form.

Eliminate the ~~truth~~ within the mind and the truth is that which remains. Consequently, remove ~~truth~~ from the mortal mind and the Eternal Mind with the consequent *ESP* events available tend to manifest automatically.

This process can be augmented by having Absolute Truths[96] or truths that are totally comprehensive in your minds storage already. When ~~truth~~

---

[96] Absolute Truths can never be removed from your mind; for the Matrix that Truth is in is the core of your existence.

is brought to Truth, it automatically dissolves into the 'special case' that it is. This is something that *Application 4* helps address.

This means that an *ESP* event can manifest automatically or naturally in two ways. When you either learn to still your mind or when a sufficient amount of Truth is programmed into your mind.

⇒ *ESP involves an interface between the Infinite Eternal Mind and your finite/temporal – mortal – mind.*

There is only One Infinite and Eternal Loving Mind. This Mind IS the very core of your being and will 'speak' to you in a way that you will understand. An *ESP* facilitated information event uses what is already within the mortal mind/matrix to convey the 'message'.

Information via the Eternal Mind – an *ESP* event -- 'clothes' the information with the mortal mind/matrix's content. The One-Mind uses recognized symbols, pictures, patterns, etc. established in and by the individual's – your -- programming and formulates a message for the mortal mind – one you will recognize.

It must do this because an *ESP* event involves an interface between the Infinite/Eternal – non-temporal/spatial -- to the temporal/spatial. The information coming through must assume temporal spatial references. Therefore, it uses the temporal spatial perceptual references already established in that temporal mind.

Or, using a swirled paint in a can analogy, dip a ball on a string into a paint can of unmixed paints – the paint is swirled with different colors. As the ball emerges, the paint patterns on the surface of the ball are those that are on the surface of the paint in the can at that moment the ball emerged.

Look at the 'paint can' as your mortal mind; the *ESP* information – the ball -- emerges and takes on swirls of 'paint' – mind's programming --from your mind as it emerges into your awareness.

As the *ESP* information came forward from the One Mind to your mortal mind, the *ESP* information is 'clothed' by your mind like the ball is clothed by the paint patterns it picked up

An excellent example of this is the original biblical 'speaking in tongues' of the Apostles.

The major government of that area, at that time, was the Roman Empire. Though Rome ruled, the 'seats of learning' in the Roman Empire were Egypt and Greece. The Roman Empire encompassed many countries and cultures; which, tended to attract people to these 'seats of learning'. Consequently, many languages were present in relatively concentrated areas.

The Apostles came from what was considered the 'boonies' – Judea -- to deliver their message to 'civilization'. They only spoke Aramaic. Yet, they could stand in the public squares and speak before a diverse crowd and each person would hear the message in their native language.

The Roman would hear the message in Latin. The Grecian would hear it in Greek. The Egyptian would hear the message in their language. The original 'speaking in tongues' was equivalent to a one way universal translating device out of science fiction.

This is an excellent instance of how Truth (outside of temporal/spatial references) becomes 'clothed' by the temporal/spatial – mortal -- mind receiving it so that mortal mind would have a reference on the information.

This is Love at work. It tends not to do something totally alien. Love is using the mental construct an individual has setup – through their own programming -- to speak through. Love uses concepts in the mortal mind to deliver the message. This way the information is usually in 'sync' with the established mortal mind's perception system. Most people do not get knocked off their ass on the way to Damascus. Even though that will occur if that is what it takes for you to grow in God.

Because *ESP* is clothed by the mind receiving it; this is why *ESP* facilities are so hard to scientifically 'nail down' – a mystery. There are so many variables that are introduced with each mortal mind's programming, perceptions/desires -- intentions, choices, etc.

This is a major variable to the 'mystery' of *ESP*. Because most people's minds are a mystery to them, an *ESP* event that is 'clothed' by their mind has mysterious elements as well.

This segues into the next concept:

⇒   *Whatever you give to Love, it will use. That means what you give to Love to grow in Love; Love will use to facilitate the process.*

Many *ESP* tools or exercises are a form of giving Love/Universe a mental construct – image or 'a set of clothes' – and letting Love speak through that image – wear the 'clothes'.

Here is an example. In one of the exercises to cultivate clairvoyance, you will construct an image. This image can be a mirror, a movie screen, a field, etc. One professional psychic teacher used the image of a flower. She would watch it grow. Then, she would ask the flower questions. What is happening with that flower would be parallel or congruent to what is happening to the person who is being 'read'.

She would begin a dialogue and question the flower, and the flower would return with the answers. If the flower is cramped, it was significant. The person is feeling cramped, closed in. She would question the flower to get parallel answers about the person while have a dialogue with this flower in her head.

The flower construct – the image -- along with a 'disinterested-interest' provided a medium for the information via the One Mind so that the information can effectively appear in a human mind (in the form the human mind set up or constructed).

ESP facilitated information can and will use these intentional mortal mind mental constructs.

⇒ *From the One Infinite and Eternal Loving Mind's reference, time and space is a 'special case', irrelevant, non-sequitar, etc.*

An *ESP* event involves an internal communion within this Eternal One Mind; and consequently, it also involves the Eternal One Mind's time/space ignor-ance.[97] The One Mind is not restricted by temporal/spatial limits, which means, <u>we can have access to everything that can be known, at any place or at any time</u>.

This One Mind is Eternally present in, and can access all of time and space; and yet the One Mind does not live in time and space. (one of those mystical conundrums to a mortal mind)

Two examples of only the time ignor-ance qualities of an *ESP* event involving elements within your mortal mind matrix and its environment it is in – *BTR*[98] -- are premonitions and déjà vu.

- ♦ A premonition is 'you' in the future, telling 'you' in the past, something is about to 'go down'.
- ♦ With déjà vu, you just accessed a future memory.

One reaches from the future to the past – premonitions – while the other reaches from the past to the future– déjà vu.

Instead of an idea shared by two apparently separate minds, déjà vu and premonitions are examples of information shared by the same mind pulled from different times.

These are two examples that are representative of an internal communication within a single mind (Mind). Both are indicative of time ignor-ance capabilities inherent in the Eternal presence of God's One Loving Mind – the Mind within you.

To summarize the preceding theory points:
- ⇨ There is only One Mind.
- ⇨ All *ESP* events involve a One Mind interaction.
- ⇨ The One Mind will use your mind's perceptual references to present the *ESP* information.
- ⇨ Temporal spatial truth references – physical laws -- are a 'special case' of the One Mind and the One Mind can ignore physical form's apparent temporal spatial sequencing.

---

[97] Chapter 3.7 - Time Ignor-ance, *I AM A I*
[98] Bubble of Temporal/spatial Reference; Chapter 3, *I AM A I*

ESP manifestation forms

How an *ESP* event makes itself known in our mortal mind can take on one or a combination of three basic forms.

1.) As a perception: words, images, etc.

2.) As emotions, body feelings, sensate (these are still somewhat perceptual, though the perceptions are less clear)

3.) Intuition, or a quiet knowing

❑ **Form 1:** *As a perception: words, images, etc.*

The first way (*form 1*) would be if the operator – you -- received the information in words, symbols, pictures, or sound. This form tends to parallel any one of your physical senses, such as vision, hearing, smelling, tasting, or sensation. These are already established perceptions within your mind. This form involves the Perception aspect of the Perception/Desire lens.[99]

This form of manifestation uses the perception aspect of your mortal mind matrix. There are so many variations of this form as there are ways to perceive. It would be prohibitive to go into them all.

How this first form works, for any one individual, will be dependent on how they have programmed their matrix -- mind. It can appear as pictures, dialogs, or monologues, complete or fractured. (The dialogue aspect is in keeping with a common perception of telepathy.)

It is also an excellent example of *ESP* using established perceptions in the mind.

❑ **Form 2:** *As emotions, body feelings, sensate* (These are still somewhat perceptual, though the perceptions are less clear – there is no 'tangible' perceptual image.)

Form 2 is another way *ESP* can appear through your *Perceptual Lens Array*. This form involves the Desire aspect of the Perception/Desire lens. This form usually manifests more as feelings -- sensate. Something may not feel right. "I've got a gut feeling." Or, "I've a very bad feeling about this." These are still somewhat perceptual, though the perceptions are less clear.

This form may be just an emotion (like fear) or it can also involve another information route, the body. In the body example, the mechanics of the information flow comes from Truth through *Storage* to the body (which makes the *ESP* information take on an 'objective event' appearance), through the 'front' of the mind using the *Perceptual Lens*

---

[99] *I AM A I*, Chapter 4.5 - The Perceptional Lens Array Matrix also *Application 7A*

Array, from Cognition through *Knowledge*, and then into our awareness in the focus buss.[100]

An important thing to recognize is the similarity of appearance of these first two types of manifestation (*form 1* and *2*) of psychic phenomena to imagination. To a mortal mind, an *ESP* event and the imagination is about as far apart as the index and middle fingers of your hand. Psychic phenomenon has a deeper feeling to it than imagination, but there can be trouble telling them apart in the beginning.

This is why caution or questioning can be important. (And, why an objective *ESP* system or tool like the *I Ching* or the *Tarot* may also be helpful.)

ESP has a slightly 'deeper' feel to it, and the information can be questioned honestly – answer seeking questions -- as much as the operator wants. The truth in an *ESP* event can withstand that questioning. It is only the ~~real~~, the ~~truth~~, which cannot stand up to honest – truthful -- questioning.

❑ **Form 3:** Intuition, or a quiet knowing.

The third form that psychic information can manifest in you is through intuition. By the term intuition this application is using the definition of intuition as a 'quiet knowing'.

With intuition there are no words, no pictures, no feelings...no perceptions. You just quietly know. Unlike the first two forms of manifestation, this form of *ESP* does not go through any of the perceptual routes – through the 'mind's eye'. It does not involve the *Perceptual Lens Array* -- 'front' of your mind -- whatsoever (as the first two forms of manifestation did). There is no 'objective' or 'subjective event' representing the 'reading'.

Intuition manifests from Truth, through *Knowledge* and bypasses the entire perceptual lens. It just occurs. It comes from Truth to the 'back' of your mind – *Knowledge* -- to you. This is the form to go for, or work with. It is the direct route. And...this is also the form that tends to occur naturally with empty mind exercises.

With the other forms, an individual can misinterpret, mislead, or introduce errors – delude oneself. The first two forms may contain perceptions and meanings attached to former irrelevant judgments or choices. This may involve *Knowledge* as well as mental/emotional sets that involve *Programming*, *Memory*, and established feedback loops as well.[101]

---

[100] Figure 4-4, Mortal Mind Matrix, back of book or *I AM A I*, Chapter 4
[101] Chapter 4, *I AM A I*

During a *form 1* or *2 ESP* event erroneous interpretations can occur or be injected.[102]

Whereas, in the case of intuition, you just know. The *Programming* and *Memory* storages are not involved as much as *Knowledge*.

It is possible to misinterpret a symbol, as with *Tarot* cards or something like that. It is very hard to misinterpret intuition, except after the fact. You can rationalize or fool yourself about what it means after the knowledge becomes present, but not when receiving the specific input. Denial is an excellent example of this.

As the first two forms (perception and sensate) are kind of parallel to perception or desire in *I AM A I*'s presented model, intuition (*form 3*) is an *ESP* form that works kind of parallel to the *Storage* interface in you. The intuition concept being presented here is an introduction to a psychic skill that does not travel through your perceptional lens – mind's eye.

Form 3 – intuition – comes naturally with empty mind exercises. This form cannot be taught; it happens as a side effect. This skill is outside of 'words'. The other two forms can be consciously cultivated however.

ESP event verification

Important: *With all three forms of* ESP *facilitated information, the operator will know 'something' is about to happen or is happening. In some other time/space line, there is an external event in* **Actual** *reality*[103] *-- physical form -- corroboration of the* ESP *acquired information.*

This corroboration between an 'objective event' and an ESP event -- 'subjective event' -- will be used as measures of successful 'readings' -- effectiveness.

With only a few exceptions, all *ESP* – One Mind -- facilitated information is true.

Most psychic readings are in reference to an objective actual event -- **Actual** reality event. So, there must be a correlation between what is happening inside your mind to outside your mind. Did it work? Did it turn out as you saw? What was different between what you saw (or what you interpreted what you saw) and the actuality, etc.? To help you recognize an *ESP* event, it can be helpful to categorize your successes or apparent successes, and failures.

As a child, the author had a strong science background. When the author first started 'playing' in his head, the author would categorize the probability of whether an experience or experiment was a success or not.

---

[102] Any perceptions based on a mistake in perception are liable to be in error as well.
[103] *I AM A I*, Chapter 4.2, 'What's Reality Papa?'

Was there a true relation between what was happening in his mind and what is happening outside of his mind?

Eventually the author saw that more than yes or no categories were needed, so the author expanded to use the following categories:

⇒ **Nothing**: the experiment did not work.

⇒ **Possible:** is a category where there <u>may</u> be a relationship between what is happening in the author's mind and what is happening outside of the author's mind. This category can include 'coincidence'.[104]

⇒ **Probable:** is a category where coincidence is not entirely ruled out; there is still no absolute confirmation of a psychic event. Reasoning may have played an important part in this category. This was especially true when the author was doing any *ESP* exercise that involves immediate perception of an external (objective) event.

⇒ **Most Probable:** is a category where the author was <u>almost</u> positive that a relationship of some sort exists between an external event and his mind/matrix. Still, the author was not completely sure.

⇒ **Definite:** usually transpired when something inside the author's mind occurred the same time that something happened in **Actual** reality. There was a direct one-to-one involvement. With some exercises, the author could actually feel something coming in or leaving him. This was especially true when working with magic

An ESP event must have a collaborating objective –physical -- correlation.

There are a few exceptions involving a critical choice and these exceptions usually involve not 'seeing' far enough; and, this is a relatively safe 'rule of thumb'. If there is no corroborating objective correlation, then the event experienced tends to be one of imagination or of mental projection; it is not an *ESP* event. And/or, the information became corrupted by the mind receiving it. Your 'subjective' and your 'objective' event must correlate, be it telepathy, clairvoyance, the use of the mind to manipulate clouds, or whatever.

You may set up different categories of success for your self. No matter what categories you set up, the **Nothing** and the **Definite** are the important ones.

---

[104] This was before the author found out that there is no coincidence. The coincidence idea is not in keeping with the idea of Absolute Love – nothing is excluded.

Be advised, teaching *ESP* is equivalent to telling you how to walk or swim. You have to do the work (and make mistakes) in order to have recognition.

Application #11A – *ESP* Experiments

This entry is a continuation of *Application 11* and contains tools for *ESP* experiments. This entry provides you with numerous options in order to cultivate a *form 1 ESP* event within you.

Exercise 11A -- Cultivating Clairvoyance, "Come along or go alone…"

As mentioned in entry *11*, *ESP form 3* – intuition – comes naturally with empty mind exercises. This form can not be taught; it happens as a side effect. The other two forms can be consciously cultivated however.

The Eternal Mind has access to everything. Every temporal mind has established internal communication symbols (perceptions). The Eternal Mind will talk in the symbols that the human mind relates to – 'clothes' itself in the mortal concepts present. It will talk in whatever symbols that have been set up in the programming, based on perceptions. It will become known in a way that is familiar.[105]

Because the Eternal Mind will talk in the symbolism that the specific mind uses, this allows for 'constructed thought systems' like *Tarot*, *I Ching*, or your own system as vectors for clairvoyance.

---

[105] *Application 11*

With this application, a thought 'system' is set up. You, the operator, are talking to this thought 'system/construct', and working through this 'system'. The Universe/Love accepts this whole symbol 'system' (symbolic matrix), and the operator is letting the symbol 'system' speak back, letting the matrices do the 'work'. However, the ideal level of clairvoyance is communion with the Universe with no mental constructs – *Form 3.*

As with previous applications, the clairvoyance exercises presented here involves some kind of motivational analysis.[106] With *ESP* applications, this is even more important.

"What is it I want from doing this? Once I find out, then what? What do I want from the exercise and from life?" "What is it I want from being psychic?"

The idea is for you to be clear, to have only one desire for the information or the question's answers. You need to pre-form your intention. You should not be concerned about the outcome: successes, accuracy, message, etc. You do not know the outcome. You just are trying to accumulate information. Doing a pre-forming of your intention, can help you clear your perceptual lens.

Cultivate a passive attitude and an open mind, and again, always a 'disinterested-interest' when doing these exercises. Do not become attached to what is happening.[107] Having a 'disinterested-interest' in most forms of communication can improve your success.

Here is something from *A Course in Miracles©* that illustrates the communion mechanism that facilitates *ESP.*

Simply do this: Be still, and lay aside all thoughts of what you are and what God is; all concepts you have learned about the world; all images you hold about yourself. Empty your mind of everything it thinks is either true or false, good or bad, of everything it judges worthy, and all ideas of which it is ashamed. Hold onto nothing. Do not bring with you one thought the past has taught, nor one belief you ever learned before from anything. Forget this world, forget this course, and come with wholly empty hands unto your God.[108]

This is, very briefly, the communion mechanism carried to the nth degree. If the word group *"wholly empty hands unto _____"* was substituted in (with _____ taking the place of the words *"your God"*), this

---

[106] *Application 7B*

[107] *I AM A I*, Chapter 5, Formula of Effectiveness

[108] A Course In Miracles, Workbook for Students, Lesson 189, *I feel the Love of God within me now.*

would be an excellent example of one-point focus listening on a mundane level.

This phrase would apply to being a good listener in a simple conversation as well as communing with God. It all depends on what your primary intent focus is -- attitude.

Group Format Application

This is a format used for an *ESP* or a mystic arts class. First, you need to pre-determine the mental construct you will use.

As mentioned in the previous series entry, one psychic teacher had a very down-to-earth way of saying how to do it, how to get in touch. All her workshops had element of being empty and still, cultivating a 'disinterested-interest', and meditating. Then she would use the mental construct idea. Her favorite image was a flower.

She would have the students first plant the flower (the seed being the person), water it, and then watch the flower grow. Watch the flower grow until it is in full bloom. When the flower is fully-grown in its maturity, the 'reader' asks it the question.

When the author first started playing with *ESP* cultivation, the author used the image of black mirror or blackboard, the pictures would unfold like a slide show. These pictures flashed momentarily on the blackboard. Whereas, with the previous example of the psychic's exercises, there is a dialogue occurring.

The idea is; for you predetermine a mental image or construct before doing this application. It can be anything; a TV screen, a pond, clouds, a blank wall, etc. Whatever communication form you will use, whether it is visual, words, images, feelings, or whatever, write down the form, the questions, and the answers when doing this application.

Remember, when you start working with this construct that you have generated in your mind and you are 'reading' somebody, you may not only ask the original question (the one on the paper), and you can also ask what this question is about. It may be important to ask what is behind this question also. How does the person who wrote down this question feel about this question?

So you are now asking more than one question about the question. There is the original question. There is also the question of what is it about this question that concerns the writer. Ask how the writer feels about this question. You are then to write down the answers that you get, from the image.

If the things that are coming to you are not clear, do not be afraid to ask the image more questions. Remember the thing about truth: it can be questioned. It will not hurt; *Esp*ecially when you are trying to learn. Be quiet, listen to what the image has to say; then, do the next question.

It is very helpful to keep the initial question precise. An example is, "If _____ does _____, what effects will this have on _____?" Precise wording aids in a precise reading.

An example of this exercise in a group setting, may be:

➢ *On two pieces of paper, everybody in the group writes down one question about their lives (or?); they are to generate two separate questions, one question per piece of paper. Do not sign it. Fold the paper up so the question inside the paper cannot be seen. Make a mark on the outside of the paper, one that you would recognize.*

➢ *All the papers go in a hat. People take turns taking a question out of the hat. They take out two questions. Look for your mark and do not take your own question. And…do not open the paper and read the question yet.*

➢ *Next, each operator pre-determines the communication image they will use. The image you create should be one you feel comfortable with. As mentioned previously, the image can be anything. It can be a flower, a blackboard, a tree, a star, a mayonnaise jar with a Funk & Wagnall's dictionary. It does not make any difference.*

➢ *Perform Application 7B; set your intention for this exercise and cultivate a 'disinterested-interest' to the application's outcome.*

➢ *After each individual has chosen their communication image and has two unopened pieces of folded paper in front of them, everybody performs a short 15-minute meditation or empty mind exercise.*

➢ *After the meditation, they then read a question on the paper.*

➢ *Then, sit with the paper in front of you, breathe and still your thoughts. Breathe; still the thoughts, while cultivating a disinterest or 0 attachment to the outcome. Then create your pre-determined construct or image in your mind with the eyes closed. Ask the construct the question; then watch and wait.*

➢ *After you generate a construct and ask questions, write down what the image says, or what you see. In a group setting, everybody would be doing this in the lab. This is being done without any communication with anyone.*

➢ *After asking the main question, ask questions that may be relevant to the main question. Example: If the main question is something like, "Why am I not happy?", ask about home-life; what makes one happy; what does make the questioner happy; etc.*

➢ *If the information is not clear, ask for more information.*

➢ *The group is given 15-minutes to do two 'readings'.*

➢ *The group comes back together and discusses some of the questions with the perceived answers.*

Individual Format Application

☐   This first exercise can be done traveling to a place that you have never been to, or it can refer to something you have never seen. Traveling will be used as an example on how to do this exercise. First, do a still mind exercise – meditate -- as stated previously. And...cultivate a 'disinterested-interest' in what you are about to do – *Application 7B.*

Do an empty mind exercise for ten-fifteen minutes beforehand. If you are traveling, close your eyes (first make sure you are not the driver) and create in your imagination a blackboard or a dark screen. Once this image is established, with your mind, take the name of the place you are going to and put it on the blackboard. Then, as a passive observer, watch the image that appears on the screen. What does it look like? Record aspects of that image in your memory. When you get to that place, compare the image you had with the actuality of the place.

Another option is to imagine driving up to the 'place' for the first time (though you had not arrived yet) and 'observe' the nature of the place as you visualize your arrival.

This is a form of distant or remote viewing.

☐   The second exercise is to use a newspaper, radio, or TV and pick a news item. It should be an item on a subject that is occurring and not concluded yet. If it is a newspaper, read the article several times, while maintaining a mental and emotional distance from the subject. It is helpful to pick a news item in which you have little or no interest. Your interest in this exercise is to 'see', not in the subject matter itself.

A return to a redundant reminder: A good part of the success of these exercises is dependent on maintaining a 'disinterested-interest' in the outcome of the 'seeing'.

After you have made yourself relatively familiar with the ideas in news item, meditate and do a still mind exercise with breathing. With your imagination, visualize an image of the news media source you got the news from. If the news media was a newspaper, imagine how the newspaper would look.

Then, with your mind, form the question: What is the outcome of this subject? Ask the newspaper, TV, radio...in your mind. Your job is to passively observe or read the results.

As in the previous applications, remember what you have read or write it down in a workbook, and keep an update on the subject through the news media or newspaper. Compare your individual reading to what actually happens; see if there is a correlation between the *ESP* event and the **Actual** reality event.[109]

This application is a form of pre-cognition.

This application consists of:
- ➤ **Meditate or do an empty mind exercise before the operation (5-15minutes)**
- ➤ **Establish your intentions and cultivate a 'disinterested-interest -- perform elements of Application 7B.**
- ➤ **Do each exercise, distant viewing and precognition, three times.**

Do not be discouraged if you do not succeed at first. The success of these exercises is dependent on several factors:

- A still mind and being.
- How well you can cultivate a 'disinterested-interest' – your non-attachment to the outcome
- How much ~~truth~~ is in your mind/matrix.
- How much *Truth* is stored in your *Knowledge*.
- How the cognitive input to *Knowledge* is used.

Learning to open your psychic perception is like learning any other skill. You may make a lot of mistakes at first or you may pick it up easy. No matter which -- to quote the *I Ching* -- "perseverance pays".

---

[109] *Application 11*

Application #12 – Cultivating Telepathy

This tool introduces telepathy theory. In this entry in the series, previous *ESP* theory is extended into a logical conclusion, telepathy. There are no exercises in this element of the series.

Exercise 12 – Telepathy theory, "choose your partner…"

The previous two elements in this series introduced the various forms in which *ESP* phenomena can appear and *ESP* cultivation. This section will focus specifically on the mechanics and aspects of telepathy.

Since all *ESP* is through the One Mind, it can be seen how *ESP* involves a communion from One mind (Mind) to another mind (yours) – a form of telepathy. All *ESP* phenomena can be 'seen' as a form of Mind/mind telepathy. This applies to a psychic seeing something in a rock, a practicing witch or shaman, to a saint in communion with God.

Telepathy, like *ESP*, is natural. Most animals have telepathic capabilities. These capabilities can be very limited in the concepts their minds work with, but telepathy is possible with animals. All life shares in the One Mind. Plants are empathic, which is a cruder form of telepathy. Plants respond to emotions. There have been all kinds of studies on the response of plants to human emotions and even studies on various means of communication between plants. How a 'stressed plant' can communicate that 'stress' to other plants for example.

Telepathy is much more common than is customarily thought. We tend not to be consciously aware of it. Or…at times, we may even be subconsciously afraid of it.

Here is an example of how common telepathy really is. Perhaps, this has happened to you at least one time or another. Let us say you are at a bus station or an airport – some group situation with strangers -- and you are not looking at anybody in particular, but you are aware of somebody over in the corner with your peripheral vision. You are just aware them and have only a mild interest.

Without moving your heads, the other person's awareness turns to you at the same time as your awareness is on him/her and there is this 'click' or a 'snap' that happens. Usually, with the 'snap', both of you will turn away at once; or, you will both turn to do something at the same time. This can be a unsettling if you dwell on it.

This 'click' is the making of a bond in which telepathy is dependent; the 'snap' is the abrupt break of the bond. If this happens in some social situation, like a bar or a party, and if communication is not shut down entirely – no 'snap', verbal or body communication can ensue.

Another example of how common telepathy is used is in a magical love spell. In thaumaturgical magic, the most powerful love spell there is consists only of a look and a touch. It is a form of telepathic bonding that is done with that look and touch.

The author has found that many women and some men already know this subconsciously without studying magic.

One definition for telepathy is an idea or ideas shared by apparently separated minds, without any physical form of communication -- BTRs[110] -- to foster that sharing. For telepathy to work, one way or another, the 'bond' is necessary. In some books, it is also called the 'love bond'. (And, remember that due to the time ignor-ance of the Eternal Mind, these two people [mortal minds] do not have to have the same temporal reference – live in the same times.)

This telepathic bond is simply a mental agreement or accord. Almost like the agreed radio frequency between a transmitter and a receiver.

It is called a 'love bond' for a number of reasons. Because Love is not exclusive,[111] it unites what <u>appears</u> to be fractured minds and beings. Love's Infinite Mind is a common thread running through the multitude of finite minds.

Another problem with words is the word *love*. The number of human projections and meanings to that word 'boggles the brain'. The bond referred to here naturally occurs when two minds develop and maintain a mild curiosity -- 'disinterested-interest'-- in each other, as in the airport or bus station example. Both individuals participating in the event are in a non-exclusive state of mind.

A bond can be just between close friends, like two buddies in the army. Under adverse situations, this bond forms between them and then these communications occur where they both know what is happening in each other's minds; it clicks. Another example is with lovers, provided they are not thinking about their projections – 'baggage' -- or other things happening in their relationship.

A Course in Miracles expresses that there are only two emotions, love or fear.[112] If you are out of fear, you are in love whether you know it or not.

The mechanics of this is ever so simple. Fear is exclusive in nature, Love is non-exclusive in nature while Absolute Love is all encompassing. At the same time, Love will not directly confront fear. With fear present, Love just will not be the major apparent influence and can appear to be absent – reside in the background. If fear is absent, Love and the Correction will automatically be present and will resume being the major influence.

---

[110] Bubbles of Temporal/spatial Reference, *I AM A I*, Chapter 3

[111] *I AM A I*, Definition of Terms -- Love: An Eternal, selfless state that is intrinsically not exclusive.

[112] Text, Chapter 13, The Two Emotions

Another way to say this is with the old axiom: Love will not enter where it is feared.

A 'disinterested-interest' works with these mechanics. A 'disinterested-interest' entails no attachments or fear, so a 'love bond' ensues naturally. Again, this 'disinterested-interest' is at the core of learning all *ESP* phenomena and at the core of most spiritual growth.

Here is an irony with ESP, telepathy, and some of the more advanced metaphysical applications. The desire to have a successful telepathic/ESP event can interfere with a successful telepathic/ESP event.

This is important and has been/will be repeated.

You must not get caught up in what you find or what you are doing. It is almost essential that you are not emotionally involved in what you discover. If you do, you can start 'losing it'. The best case scenario for this is one deludes oneself on a minor level. The worst case scenario; it may lead to psychotic episodes.

The cultivated 'disinterested-interest' tends to foster this love bond whether you know it or not, as with a stranger in the airport example. A bond ensues. When that 'snap' happens and you both turn away, that is the bond breaking.

You both have the choice whether to 'go with it' or not go with it. Turning away reflects not going with it. To act on it, you may start physically communicating through body language (like smiling) or conversation. The bond occurs first, before any ideas can be shared telepathically between the minds.

One analogy around the function of the love bond and telepathy is with the function of a *CB* radio. When using a *CB* radio, the transmitter and receiver must be tuned to the same frequency for this communication to occur. As in the *CB* analogy, it takes two to tango; both parties must have an interest – radios turned on and at the same frequency. In addition, there must be a listener and a talker; both cannot be done at the same time. So again, here is another reference to a need for the individual to learn to still themselves and become receptive – to listen.

Using this 'love bond', the individual minds do not have to think alike. The Love bond acts as if it is an automatic translating device between the individuals. That is the beauty of it. Because it works through Absolute Love, communication is translated. It goes from the perceptions of one mind and it translates over to the perceptional lens in the other's mind. The purest form of this is the speaking in tongues mentioned in *Application 11*.

There is a translation device -- for lack of a better term -- in the love bond. Once the love bond is there, Love's non-exclusive nature automatically translates. It goes from applicable knowledge in one person to another's applicable knowledge through Absolute Truth. While in each individual *Storages*, the concept being communicated is translated, clothed, or filtered through each individual's mind matrix and its programming.

It may be helpful, if both individuals have knowledge of some of the same things. Example: having mutual perceptions shared by similar cultures. A telepathic bond between a Cro-Magnon man and a New York stockbroker might be somewhat difficult, because they may not have common references, perceptions, values, wants, etc. They may not have common motivations. They may not have agreement on what is the world (a common **Individual** or **Consensual** reality[113] between them). So, it may be necessary (or desirable) some way or another to have some kind of common knowledge.

Basic human needs, emotions, and archetypes can serve as this common knowledge. It is difficult to have a telepathic bond with someone and communicate an understanding of human foibles though, if the other person does not recognize any human foibles.

To recap what telepathy needs.

♦ There has to be a love or an interest bond.
♦ You must learn to shut up and quiet your mind to listen. Be still! You must have an open mind -- no preconceived ideas. It is absolutely essential with telepathic communication, for the operator to learn to stop thinking, to still their temporal matrix. As with any form of dialogue, there is a time to listen and a time to talk. Or...with the CB analogy, if you want to listen you have to take your thumb off the transmit button.

Psychic, *ESP*, or spiritual phenomena can be broken down into two forms of telepathy -- passive and active (whether you are 'reading' or having a 'dialogue').

❑   **Passive** → Most of the psychic phenomena like clairvoyance and clairaudience tend to be on the passive side of telepathy. No specific love bond or focus is involved outside of the operator. It is more related to a 'bond' within the operator, between that human mind and the Eternal Mind, or you and your Source. One way to look at it is the operator has come to some kind of accord or agreement with the Universe or their self.

---

[113] *I AM A I*, Chapter 4.2, 'What's Reality Papa?'

How the 'bond' in passive telepathy occurs, is totally dependent on the state of mind of the individual. This means how the individual has programmed their human matrix with choices made from the information flow through the perceptual lens (*Storages*) – how much truth is already in their mind. It also involves what the individual is doing to set it up the communion, or not setting it up (the focus of the *Perceptual Lens Array*).[114]

What all the passive telepathic aspects have in common: cultivating a listening attitude, a watching and waiting, being relaxed, and paying attention with along with a 'disinterested-interest'.

Returning to the *CB* radio analogy, every thought that any person thinks is transmitted -- it is available. The volume of that transmission of perception is somewhat dependent on how much desire and emotions are involved. The stronger the desires, the stronger will be the transmission. *I AM A I* presents a vehicle analogy.[115] Desire is the fuel, whereas perception is the vehicle.

So, every thought anyone thinks is transmitted out, and the volume of that transmission is dependent on how much desire or emotion is behind it. And, because every thought is transmitted, that means passive telepathy (and active if being the receiver) involves <u>not mind reading, but mind listening.</u>

Every thought is transmitted. The individual does not have to pick things out of people's minds, because people are transmitting all the time. The operator has to learn to shut up and be discriminate about whom they want to listen to. That is an element of the bond -- a discrimination about who is being listened to.

Remember that your ability to tune into anyone's thoughts is also related to your desire. Too much desire and you will be listening to your mind instead of theirs – to what you want and those desires' perceptions. The 'disinterested-interest' mentioned helps cultivate a low-level desire (D_S = 1 or $D_S < 1$).[116] Tuning into someone specifically is dependent on how well you can be empty and have a bond with the other person. You must have enough desire to maintain an interest. But, not enough desire to generate vested interests, attachments.

The passive telepathic listener acts like radio receiver; they are turned on, are listening, and without putting anything out. Everybody is speaking at once, and the telepathic listener just happens to be a tuned listener to a specific individual. That is essentially what telepathy is all about.

---

[114] *I AM A I*, Chapter 4

[115] *I AM A I*, Chapter 4.5, The *Perceptual Lens Array*, Thought/emotion sets.

[116] *I AM A I*, Chapter 5, Formula of Effectiveness

The author used to have some problems with going into 'The City' (San Francisco) because there would be this miasma of feelings and thoughts. Nothing too specific; just 'ugh' – this murky cloud or a mental/emotional soup. The first time the author picked up on that, it threw him for a 'loop' – confusion. Such that, the author had to go back and sit up by Coit Tower for a day and until the author was used to that feeling.

This is the passive aspect of telepathy. It is telepathy through *ESP* perception. Every thought we think is transmitted. The power of the transmission can be in proportion to how much emotional charge is behind the thought. A city is full of this sea of thoughts -- other people's transmissions. With *ESP* perceptions, we tend to receive it as noise.

❏ **Active** → The telepathic act should be effortless, and not limited by time/space constraints. In having a dialogue (active form), the 'speaker' instead of thinking and having the thought go out in space (like talking to oneself), their focus is on an individual (talking to someone).

The transmission (the active part of telepathy, how much is put into somebody's mind) is dependent on the bond and the clarity of mind the sender has achieved. If there is no bond with anybody specific, and if there is strong clear thought with one emotion, it is put out into the ether -- or whatever you want to call it. It is just put 'out there'.

As with verbal dialogue, if there is to be communication, the speaker's focus must be on the awareness of the listener. Without this focus, the speaker is talking <u>at</u> someone and not <u>to</u> someone. Telepathy is similar.

To learn active telepathy is very similar to going to another country and learning a foreign language. The best way to do it is to have a companion who speaks the language. Learning comes with this daily exposure.

This partner factor helps you learn to separate **Actual** realities from the **Imaginary** realities. Observing co-relations between 'objective' and 'subjective' events gives first hand experience -- something necessary for the learning process. This correlation was touched on in *Application 11*.

In many ways, it is much better if the telepathic act is spontaneous. Rigid or controlled experiments are only useful in the beginning; they serve as introductions. Instead of setting up a time, it is much better to learn to work daily using an 'internal conversation' with another person.

And, for this book to do a lab in a group format, the only way people can really verify what is happening is if controlled experiment conditions are set up. With the case of a successful telepathic event, a specific set of conditions must be present within all people involved.

Bottom line: since telepathy involves a communication within the One Mind, telepathy is natural. It is not being telepathic that is unnatural.

The following experiments are meant to give direction. With serious study, one must learn to expand from these experiments.

Application #12A – Telepathy Experiments

This tool contains telepathic experiments. This application continues the previous series entry on telepathic theory, entry *12*. Cultivation of the bond and experimental approaches are presented here.

Exercise 12A – Bonding and telepathy experiments

A reminder: any article telling you how to develop *ESP* or telepathy is equivalent to a book telling you how to swim. Eventually, you are going to have to put the print down and get in the water and apply what you learned.

Many of the exercises in this article the author learned or 'played' with seriously while in the army. The author had plenty of time on his hands, so the author started 'playing' in his head.

When the author and his partner started working together, they rarely discussed the results; we both agreed something was happening though. Sometimes they may have orally set something up – set an experiment up; and then, they did the experiment.

Because it is a question of detached listening inside, there is no sense talking about most of the details. <u>Do it, do not talk about it.</u> Talking can cultivate attachments. Just as long as an agreement or a recognition is made, "something is happening". (In addition, there must be a correlation to **Actual** reality.[117])

---

[117] *Application entries 11, 11A, and 12*

Talking about the event can introduce all sorts of non-relevant perceptions and attachments – *Application 2*.

Remember that both people need to have the same mindset to do the operation – desire. It does not work if you want to do it and the person you work with does not want to. It does not do any good if one person's desires are focused on a computer and the other's are focused on the garden. In this case, the individuals' desires are not one and the same. You both have to have the same 'disinterested-interest'-- the same one desire to communicate. Your awareness is to be on your partner.

Part of these following experiments is for you and your partner as the operators to cultivate the same desire or interest. As the 'disinterested-interested' desires meet, the telepathic bond ensues naturally. As interests increase or the desires separate or increase in volume, it stops.

To facilitate a group lab, conditions within the lab have to be set up so that telepathy event can be perceived. One of the problems that people have with the study of telepathy is the initiating conditions are ignored or not well known.

Scientific perception assumes telepathy is mind to mind and tends to ignore the conditions in individuals' minds that set up the telepathic event or the necessity of a bond. These factors determine the effectiveness of telepathy. If people try to work with telepathy as they perceive it and they do not look at the conditions that foster telepathy, there may be problems and erratic responses.

As in physics class, the student gets theory about oscillating motion and resonant conditions and things like that. Then they go to lab and start playing with a weight and a string; they set up a set of conditions. Once they set up an experiment with a string and a weight on it, they can watch the weight go back and forth at a certain frequency (determined by the string length). Thereby, they corroborate the theory that they learned.

What is being constructed with this application/lab is that you are to first set up the conditions that foster telepathy, then try to get at least some experience within a group setting or a paired setting of telepathy occurring; to see that it is possible that telepathy can occur.

For the lab in a group situation, the group would first meditate for fifteen to twenty minutes, and then people would pair up with a partner. Avoid pairing with somebody you have a very strong interest in, either positive or negative. (Meaning, do not hook up with anybody because you want to get into his or her pants.) At the same time, do not hook up with somebody you have some aversion to or you have some negative feelings about. No strong interest, either positive or negative. The idea being presented here is to keep your individual desires and attachment levels down.

Before the experiment can start, a bond has to occur between the two participants, Especially if it is not there when they first pair up. A set of conditions <u>has</u> to be cultivated for the telepathy experiment to work.

There are a number of ways to approach this bond concept:

- ❏ One way to do it is to sit facing each other, not touching and <u>not looking</u> at each other. Be empty and mentally aware of the other's presence in front of you.
- ❏ Another way is to sit next to each other (side by side and touching) and visually looking at the same thing and be aware of each other's presence.
- ❏ Another way is to sit back to back and be aware of each other's presence.
- ❏ Another is to do a five-minute breathing exercise together. Then, get up and slowly walk around the room while always being aware of the presence of the other wherever you are in the room. Do this for 2-3 minutes, then sit down and do the exercise.

Whatever approach used, you need to be aware of the other's presence and breathe into this awareness.

As mentioned, there are so many ways to approach this. The first examples given do not include any direct eye contact. However, the experiment participants can try using direct eye contact.

- ❏ One example is a condition where the individuals sit facing each other, knees touching. They just sit, and look into each other's eyes. They could do a one point focus exercise with the other person's eyes as the focal point, and breathe into it or just look into each others eyes momentarily.
- ❏ Another way is to have each one take their right hand, look into each other's eyes and touch the cheek of the other one at the same time. That is, to use a physical symbolic action to help foster the bond.

A mental bond can ensue so many ways. These are just suggestions to a few ways it could be consciously nurtured.

Both experiment participants need to look at their desires or fears, and recognize that they have an internal movie. They have desires around their perception of the group and the exercise itself. These perceptions/desires can, and will, interfere with the internal telepathic mechanism.

As with all latter previous exercises, a pre-forming of intention is appropriate, if not essential.[118]   Remember to ask yourself something equivalent to...

- What do I want from this exercise?
- What is my motivation/intention for sitting and doing this?
- How do I see this group/person?
- What do I want from this group/person?
- What do I want when am I doing this exercise?

The ideal is to establish a motivation (one desire) where you are doing it because you want to learn.   You want to grow.   You want to communicate.   You want to expand yourself.   Having no preconceived thought or perception is very appropriate if you do not know where you are going.   It does not get in the way of 'getting there'.   Recognize your ignorance.

The beginning of this application involves being still, sitting and breathing, and being empty together.   Just wait, and be aware of that other person.   The purpose is to calm your mind and develop a 'disinterested-interest' to communicate one way or another with this person.

In the group scenario, participants would do a bonding exercise for 5-10 minutes.   Remember; no thought is appropriate.   If you have thoughts: "I don't want to think about that now"; or "I want to do this exercise instead." Breathe into waiting with that person.   It is essential to cultivate the 'disinterested-interest' in communicating to that person.

Before performing the experiment, the two individuals agree on who will be a transmitter and who will be the receiver.   For a short time, one experiments as a transmitter; while, the other experiments in receiving. After doing a few experiments, you are to exchange roles.

Next is to break out the playing cards.   Playing cards are given to the transmitting people in the group.   If there are 10 people – 5 pairs, each transmitter has 10 or more cards.   For small groups or a single pair, do not use the whole deck; use only a handful of cards.[119]   Both people – receiver and transmitter -- should look at the cards chosen[120] and then the transmitter takes the cards.

The transmitter shuffles the cards.   The transmitter will use the short stack of cards before them as a record of the cards and their sequence.

There are several ways for the 'transmitter' to approach this exercise:

---

[118] *Application 7B*

[119] It may help facilitate successful experiments if the cards were visually dissimilar: a male face card, a female face card, a red ace, a black ace, a red ten, a black eight, etc.

[120] This way the receiver's mind has relevant information to work with.

⇒   **Option number one** is the transmitter holds a card. As the two experimenters face each other, the transmitter looks at the card and rotates it around <u>in their mind</u>, looking at the front and back.[121]

Visualize the card in their mind; and look at what impact the card has to them. You can use symbolic meaning, like the words, 'King of Hearts' while doing this. The transmitter can cultivate the image of the King of Hearts in their mind. First, the transmitter is aware of what they are doing inside their mind with this picture of King of Hearts. Then they look at the receiving person, using their imagination, and place that perception they have of the card into the receiver's head or on the forehead.

⇒   **In the second option**, the transmitter physically looks down at that card and gets a perception in their mind of the card. Then, they look up at the other person, use the awareness of connection, and act like they are "telling' them the card in the mind. Alternatively, the transmitter acts inside themselves as if they already have communicated the idea. Sit with the other person with the conviction that you both know what the card is – as if you just said it.

The first example is taking the thought and putting it into the other's mind. The other example is recognizing a bond and letting the bond do the work. This can be looked at as an attempt for two minds to think the same thought at once. It may help if the sender imagines you are one mind, and you both think this thought and have the image of the King of Hearts at the same time.

The receiver's job is to sit and wait, be totally passive with a 'disinterested-interest', and to breathe slowly. Remember this is only an experiment. Nothing of value is at stake. Minimize your attachments to success on this exercise.

As if waiting for that person to say something, the receiver is sitting and waiting. Again, it cannot be stressed enough -- cultivate a 'disinterested-interest' in the desire to know what the card is. Have no fear. If you experience fear, just breathe into it and let it go. The receiving person's awareness is on the person in front of them; then, says or writes the first image that comes in their head.

What may or may not help is for the receiver to be aware of the person before them and visualize a blank card, a card with no markings on the front. Then let the card color itself in.

---

[121] Similar to *Applications 6* in this series, time and space visualization applications

The transmitter keeps track of which cards were used (and what order) in the card sequence. The receiver will keep track of what they are receiving and in what order in a notebook or on a piece of paper. Then, after the exercise, the two experimenters compare. Do this several times, then switch roles. The receiver becomes the transmitter and vice versa.

One-sided successes reflect that someone was passive. A recurring event that showed up when doing these experiments in a group format was the listener may actually be 'reading' the deck of cards and saying what the next card in the deck was rather than listening to the transmitter – no bond.

Having successful comparisons definitely reflects a two-way communication, facilitated by a bond (and usually you both already know it). If one person is successful, it only tends to mean that one person may be more 'in tune' to the 'psychic' than the other and has more of an awareness of the cards. Because telepathy is natural, this infers they may have less of an interest in the success of the experiment

Again, non-attachment to the outcome cannot be overstressed. Your very desire to want to do this and have some success can get in the way of having any *ESP* success. This again reflects back to the formula of effectiveness.[122] If your desires and attachments start to rise, then your effectiveness is going to go down.

Yet another return to a redundant reminder:
Attachments to a successful telepathy event can interfere with a successful telepathic event.

In conclusion, your practice will increase your success rate. There are many different options to how you can play with the presented concepts. This series entry is just giving some basic guidelines. Experiment participants can speed up or slow the rates of how they have contact with the cards as they start to get a feel for what is happening. It can become more spontaneous.

This application consists of:
- ➢ *Find a partner.*
- ➢ *Both cultivate a 'disinterested-interest' and pre-form intentions – Application 7B.*
- ➢ *Decide ahead who will be transmitter and who will be the receiver.*
- ➢ *Assemble the cards*
- ➢ *Both participants meditate beforehand.*
- ➢ *Do a 'bond' exercise, develop the 'bond', or its conditions.*
- ➢ *The transmitter looks at the card 'communicates' the card to the receiver.*

---

[122] *I AM A I*, Chapter 5, Formula of Effectiveness

- ➢ *The receiver writes what they perceived.*
- ➢ *The transmitter goes through the stack of cards keeping them in order.*
- ➢ *After going through the stack of cards, the receiver compares their notes to the card stack order.*
- ➢ *Do this; and then, transmitter and receiver reverse roles (transmitter → receiver and receiver → transmitter) and do the exercise again.*
- ➢ *Discuss perceptions afterward and perhaps make some entries in a journal.*
- ➢ *Do this on three separate occasions, preferably on different days and at different time of day.*

Application #13 – Sound of Music

Music is the most powerful spiritual/metaphysical tool that Man has. This entry in the series combines previous applications to show how listening to music affects your mind, along with, providing you with numerous application directions.

Exercise 13 – Music exercise variations, "riding the music"

The true power of music lies in the mind of the listener or the musician – your mind.[123] And, who you really are is way beyond the music. The music itself is only a tool.

Listening to music can involve a number of mental applications already introduced in previous series entries. These applications are:

---

[123] This application will not concern itself with the "Music of the Spheres' concept – the Universal music.

1) *Application 5*: Eye Exercise or 'Surfing' the Mechanism
   a) In this application, as the eye and the mind coordinate, the information of the event goes through the mind's cognition mechanism and it takes a specific moment of time as it does so. Your mortal mind/matrix is refocusing. Constantly moving the eyes before the cognition mechanism is completed, creates a condition of non-choice and no 'subjective event' in the mind/matrix.[124] Your mind/matrix is constantly refocusing before it finishes a recognition cycle. When listening to music, you are doing the eye-exercise with your ears. Your mind is constantly refocusing on each note. You are 'seeing' with the ears while you are resetting your mind.
   b) The result of doing this for just a short period of time is your mind/matrix starts over after you are done – resets.[125] Herein is a major effect of listening to music; it is a release or stepping out of the mental processes. Music helps you take your mind off of your woes. This is how music can be cathartic
   c) Due to the above, listening to music for an extended period of time can initiate trance states, like long distance driving.

2) **Meditation *Applications 8-10***
   a) Meditation is a one-point focus on an event. Listening to music is a one point focus on an event.
   b) Previous applications – *Application 10* -- stated that it is hard to keep an empty mind or a blank mind indefinitely. However, it is much easier to do the blankness in short 'bursts'. Rather than to keep an empty mind and do it for 5 or 10 minutes, it is easier to do 'bursts' of blank, blank, empty, empty, empty.
      i) When first emptying the mind, there is a focus on an initial effort to have an empty mind; and then, a focus on maintaining the emptiness. These repetitive 'bursts' can be seen as a repetitive initial effort (as opposed to making the effort to be empty and holding it).
      ii) In *Application 10* the idea was introduced that with chanting and some meditations, you can use the words as the vehicles for this emptiness or blankness. With instrumental music, you can introduce the emptiness or blankness with each note, sets of notes – chords, or beat.
   c) With the case of music involving a singular instrument, the emptiness can also be initiated <u>between</u> the notes. This can also be done with multiple instruments and following a melody. Your mind introduces 'bursts' of emptiness between the notes of the

---

[124] The Cognition path is a high priority survival loop. It takes precedence over many other mental processes. When it is in operation, other mental operations cease.
[125] *Application 5*

melody. You can use the notes and words. Either way, listening to the music serves as a vector to a one point focus -- meditation.

    d) Be advised, that repetitive use of the mind's focus on emptiness is a similar use of the mind as the eye exercise already mentioned (a repetitive cognitive operation). It is also similar to the quick repetitive use of a word as was introduced with meditation entries to the series – Transcendental Meditation. And still…a one-point focus of performing this act/event <u>makes this a meditation</u>. All of the above is combined in one operation – listening to music.

3) _Applications 1A_ and _4_, the effect truth has within the mind

    a) Previous applications in this series have mentioned that truth has an effect on the mind. From _Application 1A_ -- a passive activity -- to 'pumping' truth through the mind or weaving thought forms like Lexio Divino[126] – an active application, Truth can alter consciousness. Taking the two previous examples of how music can alter consciousness through a constant reset and having a one-point focus for a window of time (a delta t -- Δt), 'pumping' truths – concepts -- through that same altered mind will augment the effect of the previous two conditions.

    b) This is the power of musical verse. The one-point focus on the words of the music serve the same purpose as the one-point focus on the words of a chant. In addition, it introduces to the mind a sequence of concepts that will alter consciousness depending on how much Truth (and individual associations to the Truth) is in these concepts. This is called weaving thought forms.

4) _Application 4_ and Chapter 2 _I AM A I_, introduced how a logic system can create something 'alien' to that logic system…

    a) Previous series entries introduced the idea that the concepts of infinite--finite or eternal--temporal are mutually exclusive. Anything created which is not of a finite temporal mind – mortal mind, must be automatically infinite and eternal related.

    b) As with _Application 5_, the mortal mind can be used to step out of mortal mind activity; it can do this by using eternal concepts.

5) What ever you give to Love, Love will use.

    a) There are many ways to build a house. Yet, every house must obey the laws of physics – of matter or **Actual** reality.

    b) This God's Love arrangement allows us to custom design our own spiritual trip. Religious contemplatives agree; all spiritual journeys work with the same internal mechanics. Many contemplative orders – monastic orders -- basically say you have to do the same things, perform similar internal operations. The individual involved is just changing the mental constructs – paradigm or philosophies -

---

[126] _Application 10C,_ Option 2

- they are using and the applications' forms. The end is the same; the basic mental internal operations are similar. Love dictates that we will be aware of our union with God. It is a closed system.[127] It is only a question of time (which, does not exist from an Eternal Love's reference).[128]

An example of the effects of combinations of all the above is gospel music. The mind is primed by listening to the instrumental and rhythm; then, spiritual concepts are pumped through the mind.

In the instance of gospel music, prayers or heart-songs -- bursts of heart or emotional energy united with a perception/idea/concept (as opposed to a burst of an empty mind) -- are put to music.

Please note; that the song length can act as your timing device. In this way, the song acts like the kitchen timer used in the meditation exercises. The music itself – song length – automatically becomes your objective time keeping mechanism mentioned in previous applications.

As with the meditation exercises, setting aside this specific time window for an application can help bring your focus back. "I am going to do this exercise or operation until the song (or album) is over."

In summary, because multiple internal events can be involved with the music tool, there can be numerous music application directions – modalities -- that can be taken.

Internal Applications (Non-physical)
❑   With this exercise and its passive use of music, each note is accompanied with focus and blankness.

For the beginner, this application may be easier to learn if you do an empty focus with only instrumentals. That way there are no words to distract or to initiate any mentation.

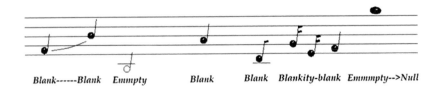

Blank------Blank   Emmpty   Blank   Blank   Blankity-blank   Emmmpty-->Null

With instrumental music, as introduced previously, you can introduce the emptiness or blankness with each note or sets of notes -- chords.

---

[127] Due to God's All Encompassing Love.
[128] From the Eternal reference, the 'awakening' has already happened.

The idea that it is hard to keep an empty mind or a blank mind indefinitely has been introduced. However, it is much easier to do the blankness in short 'bursts'. Rather than to keep an empty mind and do it for 5 or 10 minutes, it is easier to do 'bursts' of: blank, blank, empty, empty, empty.[129]

As stated in *2b* previously, when first emptying the mind, there is an initial effort to have an empty mind. Then there is an effort to hold the mind empty. These repetitive 'bursts' can be seen as the recurring effort to initially empty the mind.

In addition, the previous meditation exercises – *Applications 8-10* -- introduced the idea that with chanting, you can use the words as the vehicles for this emptiness or blankness – *2a* above.

Variations of this application are:

⇨ Emptying the mind between notes
⇨ Slowly breathe and you ride the music out. All you are doing, is riding out each note, existing quietly, waiting and being patient, and being empty until the song is done.
⇨ You can use the words as the vehicles for this emptiness or blankness as was introduced with the idea of chanting,

In all of the above applications and if you are working with instrumentals, no thought is appropriate in your mind until your music operation is done.

External Applications (Physical)
Listener
Any physical application – external -- will be an extension of an internal operation.

❑ Dance is an excellent tool of extending the internal state into an external state. As the mind is stilled, the music is allowed to move through the mind into the body with out thought -- mentation.

Musician
❑ As with any element of the internal applications mentioned previously, the musician is like their instrument before it is picked up to be played – still and empty. When the instrument is picked up to be played, just as they are playing the instrument, the 'music' is playing them.

"They're a band beyond description,

---

[129] You are using *Application 5*'s continual cognition refocusing; you are refocusing to emptiness.

Like Jehovah's favorite choir.
People join hand in hand.
While the music plays the band,
Lord they're setting us on fire."[130]

As mentioned, for the beginning listener, it may be easier to learn to do an empty focus with only instrumentals. That way there are no words to distract or to initiate any mentation. The author first learned this exercise with jazz and long rock and roll instrumentals.

As it has been introduced, there are numerous modalities of using music as a meditation aid. Many of them are variations of some of the previous applications already presented in this series. The intention of this series entry is to introduce the concept – music tool -- to you and have you do (or devise) your own exercises. .

This application consists of:
> *This application is for you to pick four pieces of instrumental music (one preferably involving drums). The pieces should be ten to twenty minutes long.*
> *Find a place where you will not be disturbed and get in a comfortable (but not too comfortable) position.*
> *Do a short period of slow deep breathing, set your intention for this exercise – Application 7B, turn the music on, and enter.*
> *Focus on emptiness, or if you use effort, a re-occurring 'blankness' of mind with each instrumental note.*
> *Do this once for each piece of music*
> *After each exercise, sit and be still for several minutes, and notice any thoughts or sensations and perhaps record them in a notebook or journal – Application 7B again.*

> *Optional Application 1, Do the above application; then, physically dance to the music to a second piece of music. As the mind empties to the music, your body is moving to it (or in it) – extend the stillness within you into movement.*
> *Optional Application 2, If you are a musician, pick a song you know well and do not allow any mentation – no thought – as you are playing for the entire length of the piece. Be as empty on the inside as your instrument is empty of sound before you pick it up.*

Starting with drums can be helpful as a beginning choice. Sit or lie in a relaxed position and, first, do the passive application of focus to music. This should be done for at least fifteen minutes

---

[130] Lyrics by John Barlowe, *The Music Never Stopped*, Blues For Allah, The Grateful Dead, Copyright 1975 by Ice Nine Publishing, Inc.

It should be mentioned that music's effect can work on an individual level or a group level. All of the above affects can become augmented when done on an assembled group level; specifically, with live music. The idea of using music to produce group mind focus and emptiness is at the core of all religious use of music, from shamanic use of drums, to musical religious chants (e.g. Gregorian), to church choirs, or to a 'Dead' concert.

Eliminate ~~truth~~ and there is only Truth. If a group of people is doing the same things in their mind (music effects stated previous) and no ~~truth~~ is enforced or re-enforced within that window of time on a group level, Truth is what remains. Because of this, a secular music event can turn spiritual without warning.

"Once and a while you can get shown the light, in the strangest of places if you look at it right."
Scarlet Begonias, Grateful Dead.

This cannot be stressed enough: Until you take your daily internal disciplines into everyday life -- whatever disciplines you have -- it will not mean a thing. You need to learn to 'take it to the street'.

Application #14 – Through You

This is a tool that allows you to perceive how energy flows. Using previous applications, this is an introduction to energy flow through your body using your hands.

Exercise 14 – Energy, just passing through

This exercise is short and sweet. It involves some body awareness as well as some mental awareness. Sit in a comfortable position with your hands resting on your knees; your wrists resting on the knees with the hands hanging over the knees. The palm of your right hand should be facing up – "to Heaven", while the palm of your left hand should be facing down – "to earth". Your hands themselves should not be touching any object.

Slowly breathe for a few minutes and relax. As you are doing this, notice how you feel. Notice how the energy in your body, arms, and hands feel. Alternatively, another option for this application is to place your awareness on your hands; notice how the space – a cubic inch space -- just outside of your palms feels. How that space feels.

Relax, breath, and slowly get a feel for this position for a minute or two; and then, quickly reverse your hand positions. Your right hand palm is now down, while the palm of the left hand is facing up. Quickly flip your hands positions and notice the change you feel inside and what that change feels like.

Now…sit with the hands in the reverse position for a minute or two – left hand up and right hand down -- and notice what this feels like (or what you feel outside the palms). After a few moments of observing again flip your hands quickly while noticing the changes you feel.

This application consists of:

➢ **Do this twice (four flips) at least three different times and allow at least 1 minute of time between flips to accumulate observations.**
➢ **Notice and/or record any changes you perceived in how flipping your hands felt in your journal.**

This exercise is related to why the *Mage* (Major Arcana *Tarot* card *1*) has his right hand to Heaven while his left is to earth.

Road Signs and Series Conclusion

"What was that?!"

Effectiveness has been mentioned throughout this toolkit. In some instances, effectiveness of some of the continual applications may be 'road signs'. Some common signs, states of consciousness, or experiences – road signs -- can be introduced.

Many of these 'signs' that can occur are an effect to some of your exercises. Some can occur shortly after you start do exercises and be like a quantum leap. While others are results of long-term mind/matrix reprogramming.

All are like road signs on a journey. All should be 'looked' on as such and then keep 'moving on'. Preoccupation with a road sign can detract from the 'trip'. If you are busy watching a road sign, you are not looking where you are going; you may not see the cow in the road.

Some of these 'signs' are such that if you change your focus from what your exercise or operation is to the 'sign', the 'sign' disappears. This is because the sign is a side effect to what you are doing.

Everything that has been presented in this toolkit initiates changes in your mortal mind/matrix mechanics and you may experience consciousness changes or have effects from them. Every mortal mind/matrix is like a snowflake. Even though every snowflake may be different, yet there are numerous elements they have in common.[131]

---

[131] Water matrix (molecule), the nature of solid matrix created by a series of water matrices (molecules) when at a specific conditions: temperature, an impurity, relative humidity, etc.

Your mortal mind/matrix may experience variations of changes. Even though those changes are along the same set of laws/truths each can manifest a variation in form like the snowflake.

These changes/signs are arranged here into three specific categories. These categories are, basically, reflections of postulated qualities of Chapter 2. The second postulate (God's Love) forms one category and is 'heart' related. The third postulate (God's Logical Mind) forms a second category and is 'mind' related. And, since they are One, a third category is formed as a combination of 'head' and 'heart'.

Most of these may mean nothing to you. Some of these signs you may understand only after you experienced them.

1) Head
    a) Epiphanies or sudden quantum mental jumps into metaphysical or spiritual subject concepts
        i) An intense sense of beauty related to the 'whole'
        ii) These also can instigate heart states
        iii) Mount of Transfiguration' a major epiphany that involves exposure to the Absolute Power of God.
    b) Deep meditation states
        i) A perceived light that appears while doing a mental exercise for a period of time
            (1) A light forming in the mind while in a deep meditative state
            (2) A light forming in the mind while in a deeper meditative state than a. This light has a dark spot or 'door' in the center of it.
        ii) Derivatives of the 'Precious Stillness' within the Eternal Moment of Creation
            (1) Several forms of a peaceful contemplation
            (2) The "velvet monkey wrench" – you are incredibly soft surrounding 'that' which is still and immovable.
        iii) A visual blackout that occurs while doing an exercise for a period with open eyes and all 'visual' perception disappears (or maybe just the peripheral).
    c) An introduction to the 'Dreamtime' or psychic education (*ESP* validation)
    d) A blinding white light
        i) Getting "knocked off your ass on the way to Damascus"
        ii) Usually associated with some initiation or initiatory process
2) Heart
    a) A 'bliss-out', a variety of states that comes with maintained prayer (heart-song)
        i) The Bodhisattva Choice

    ii)   The Absolute Love behind the 'Mount of Transfiguration' – The Power
  b) Bodhisattva heart flame
3) Combination
  a) A 'bliss-out' that comes with an epiphany
    i)   Compassion
    ii)   Intense 'heart' spaces accompanied by holistic perceptions
  b) Bodhisattva tears

You should know it is a mistake to look for these or after experiencing them give them excessive meaning. These are effects of the 'work' and should be looked on as such. "Oh that's kind-a neat!" Then, move on. Becoming preoccupied with the 'effects' can cause you to be distracted from the work that is the 'cause'.

Or, as it is written, "My Father's house has many mansions." Don't get lost in the 'rooms/mansions'.

Conclusion

The term 'mortal mind' is used a lot in this toolkit. This is a reference to your whole mortal being – both mind and heart. The paradigm that is presented with these exercises presents the mind and heart as being one thing.[132] They are the 'flip' sides of the same coin (*Application 7A*). A change of heart effects a change of mind. A change of mind effects a change of heart. They are one thing. This is a mortal variation on God's Infinite Eternal Mind and Love being One thing.[133]

"The map is not the terrain." The model of *I AM A I* presents a an operational map or flow chart; it is the exercises in *I AM A I* the *Truth Tuning Toolkit* that introduces to you the 'terrain' of your mind or being. A map is only important in that it gives you an objective reference to a journey. It is in the application of the concepts presented by the map – the steps – that gets you to your destination.

You can put a bunch of physicists in a room and have them discuss and 'crunch numbers' around gravity and Newton's Laws of Motion all day. And…until they apply them, "They ain't walking out of that room."

Application is everything.

"A journey of a thousand miles begins with a single step."
Tao te Ching

---

[132] *I AM A I*, Chapter 4
[133] *Postulate 3*, God's Absolute Love has an Absolute, Logical, and Eternal Mind. -- *I AM A I*, Chapter 2

This series presents you with a set of application tools only.

- Given: you are the Beloved of God.
- Then: anything you do is a tool to help you remember who you really are.

Once you remember, the tools may not be necessary.

This toolkit has exposed you to the mechanics of your mind. Variations and combinations of these exercises can be found in any serious mystically orientated spiritual philosophy. Elements of these exercises are found (and are practiced) in the contemplative element of all world religions.

These religious practices may involve some aspect of:

⇒ There is a Divine 'Something Else'.
⇒ Truth can affect your being
  - Perceiving truth has any affect
  - Pumping truths through the mind
⇒ The importance of not doing something
  - The importance of decreasing or 'tweaking' desires
  - The importance of non-attachment – a disinterested-interest
⇒ One-point focus on an event
⇒ Extending your perceptions beyond that which is around you – seeing further
⇒ Importance of intention
⇒ Exercising the mind
⇒ The use of music

Because the paradigm used in this book is science orientated – empirical, application of the truths/laws in the paradigm will enhance your personal life independently of whether you have a spiritual belief system. Your perception will expand.

This is simply because you are using your mind on a more comprehensive level.

The Peace of God is with you; it never left you.

RELEVENT ILLUSTRATIONS

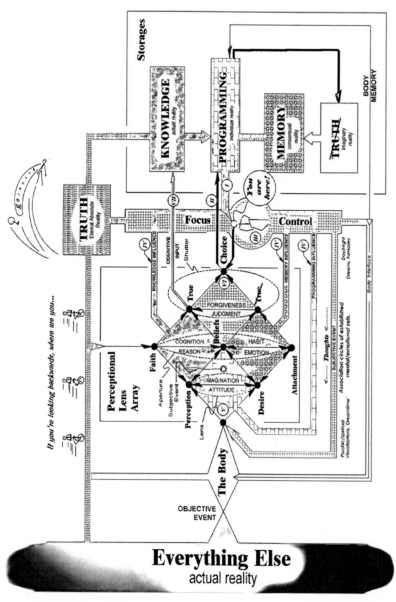

Figure 4-4, Mortal Mind Matrix

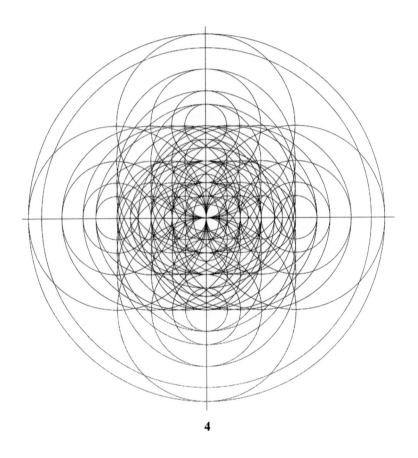

4

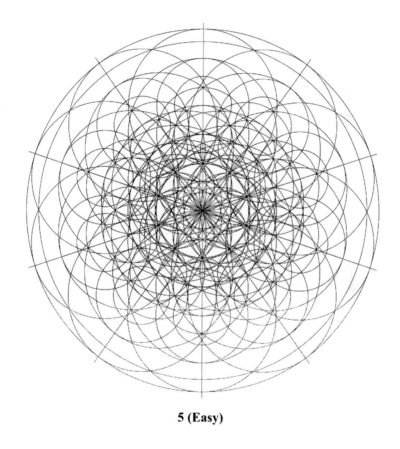

5 (Easy)

5 (Hard)

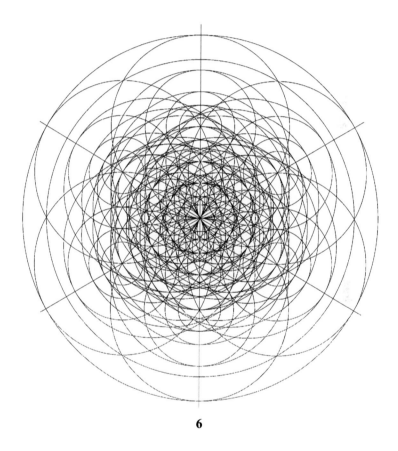

6

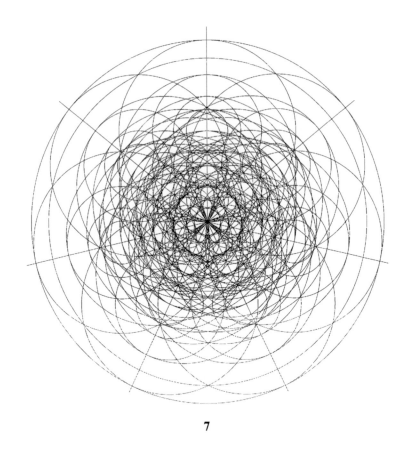

7

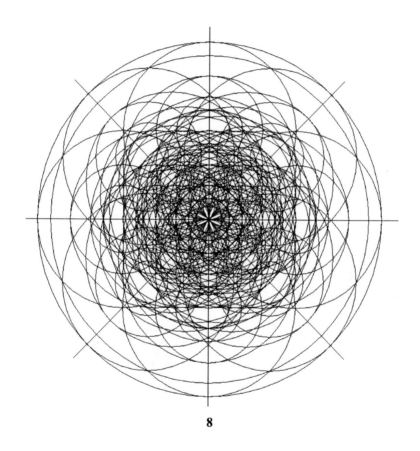

8

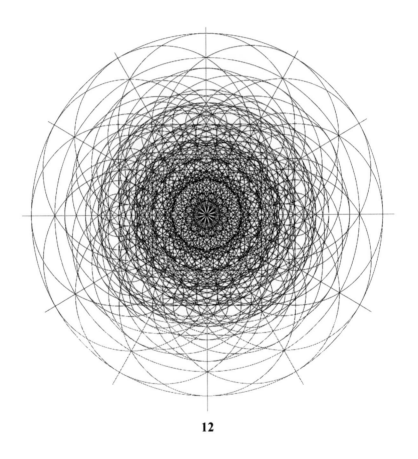

12

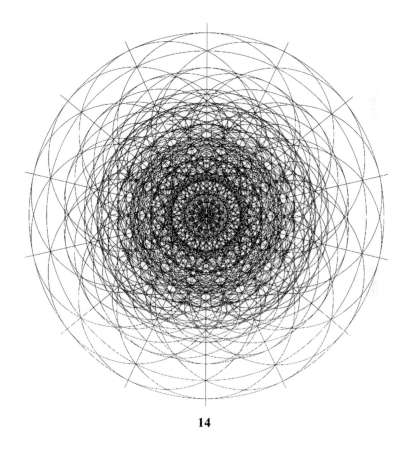

14

We Have Met
the Enemy
and He Is
Us

(Pogo, aka Walt Kelly)

150

About the Author

When the author was very young, he would take toys apart to see what made them work. As he got older, he turned that inquisitiveness to how his mind worked. Between the ages of 9-18 he learned or started 'playing' with a multitude of things such as: he could not trust his mind; the relationships of wants – desires – in everything we do (and changing his desires); he learned the permanence of mathematics and science; there were 'glitches' in our – Mankind's -- perception of reality; he learned blank mind exercises -- "Can I stop thinking"; he learned truth perception in everyday objects; he learned to use music to aid blank mind exercises; and, he started to experiment with entering deep relaxation trance states.

The ages of 18-20 found Steven as a merchant seaman and he sailed the pacific orient for a while before the selective service caught up with him. When a seaman, he learned about chanting and would do this on the deck of the ships he sailed and he also 'played' more with various trance states.

He entered the army at the age of twenty. The author turned the army experience into a serious metaphysical study and mental practice; mostly as a rebellion to the army ("They got my body, but they don't have my soul.") He began studying and doing exercises regularly in the *Tarot, I Ching*, thaumaturgical magic, music aided exercises, and learned raja yoga. Steve devised and performed numerous empirical experiments in the mystical/*ESP*/magic vein at this time and did many while he was doing his military chores

It was while in the army he was initiated into an intense period of internal schooling of thirteen months, which had distinct transitions/initiations through the 'schooling'. The schooling continued after his release from the army. The graduation from this school required his death. The age of twenty-three found Steven as a fourth level initiate, an adept.

Thinking it could not be that simple, he then studied the core concepts of world religions. The author found he could pick up books like *Tao te Ching, Upanishads*, or *Bhagavad Gita* and the majority of the time knew exactly what the books were expressing.

He has been in service to communities dedicated to growth, education, service, or of a spiritual nature most of the time since then. Fixing things is his version of "chopping wood and carrying water". The spectrum of these communities range from years working at Esalen Institute to years working for a Catholic monastery. Consequently, he has been exposed to a multitude of philosophies and thought systems.

He has taught workshops in *Mysticism and the Moody Blues, Magick: Preparation of the Operator*, and was a *Course in Miracles©* group discussion leader for a number of years. In addition, he has regularly taught an extracurricular quarter class titled an Introduction to the Mystic Arts (or Science) class at Heartwood Institute.

In addition he has invented two virtual photon devices, an electric field transformer and a virtual photon power converter.

In the summer time, Steven can be found attending outdoor music festivals, applying *I AM A I*'s concepts.

CPSIA information can be obtained at www.ICGtesting.com
Printed in the USA
BVOW01s0001120914

366481BV00001B/41/P